Contents

Foreword

The Great Glen Way runs for 77 miles (124 km) from Fort William to Inverness. It starts beside Britain's highest mountain, Ben Nevis; follows its greatest geological fault along the shores of its most famous loch, Loch Ness; and finishes at Inverness, its most northerly city and the capital of the Highlands. Much of it goes alongside the Caledonian Canal, Thomas Telford's far-sighted feat of Victorian engineering that opened in 1822.

Most of the route is straightforward, with flat sections along canal towpaths and some disused railway trackbed, and undulating parts on forest tracks and minor roads. However, there are some demanding gradients and terrain, and the final section is a challenging 20 miles
(32 km) long: see page 7.

Since its royal opening in 2002, the route has evolved into a number of Great Glen Ways for people to enjoy by various means. Although at first there was a Great Glen Cycle Route that diverged from the walking route, the distinction was abandoned in 2006, since when the whole route officially could be biked or hiked. Most people walk the route in five to seven days or cycle it in two to four days. Others enjoy it on horseback or paddle it in a canoe: the well-established Great Glen Canoe Trail attracts thousands of paddlers each year.

In 2014, through a £1 million project, the Forestry Commision Scotland created over ten miles (16 km) of waymarked Great Glen 'High Route' above Loch Ness. This takes you above the tree line and offer much better views than the traditional route, with some challenging gradients and a new summit at 422 m (1385 ft) on Creag Dhearg. We believe that this option has made the Way one of the finest of Scotland's Great Trails.

Across Loch Lochy to two Munros: see page 27

Great Glen Way

Walk or cycle the Great Glen Way

Jacquetta Megarry
and Sandra Bardwell

Rucksack Readers

About the authors

Sandra Bardwell
A dedicated, lifelong walker, Sandra worked in Australia as archivist and historian, and wrote extensively about bushwalking and national parks. Settled in Scotland since 1989, she has written guidebooks for Lonely Planet, Sunflower Books and Rucksack Readers.

Jacquetta Megarry
A professional author turned publisher, Jacquetta devised the weatherproof Rucksack Readers format after discovering the joys of long-distance walking. She has since written or co-authored 19 guidebooks in the series.

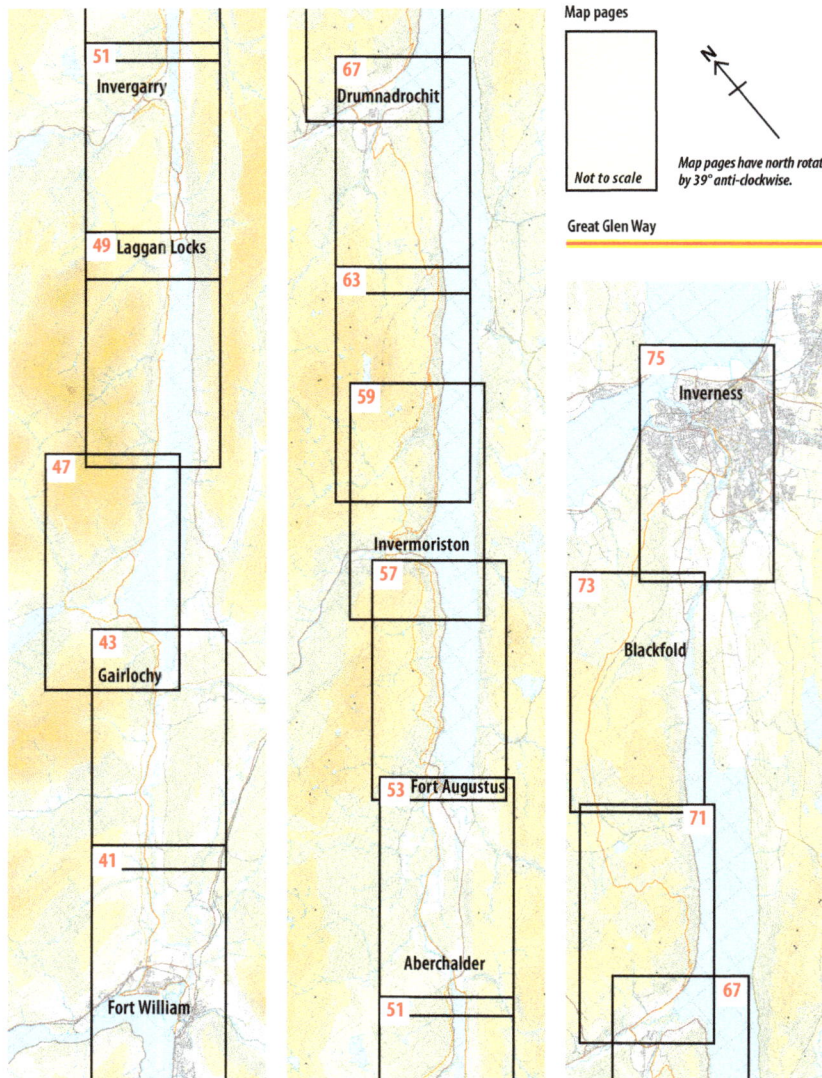

Map pages

Not to scale

Map pages have north rotated by 39° anti-clockwise.

Great Glen Way

51 Invergarry

49 Laggan Locks

47

43 Gairlochy

41

Fort William

67 Drumnadrochit

63

59

Invermoriston

57

53 Fort Augustus

Aberchalder

51

75 Inverness

73 Blackfold

71

67

1 Planning and preparation

The Great Glen Way is a very appealing route, one that any healthy person of any age can tackle and realistically expect to complete. t is slightly easier than the West Highland Way, for example, being shorter overall, less strenuous and mainly on better terrain. Consistent waymarking and generally modest gradients also make this route a good choice for your first long-distance route.

Planning and preparation are important. Well in advance, complete a few long hikes or bike rides, depending how you intend to travel. Progressively build up the distance that you complete, and try to go out on consecutive days. While training, carry a realistic load on your bike or in your rucksack. Inexperienced walkers can obtain our *Notes for novices*: see page 79. Cyclists should observe the SNH leaflet *Off-road cycling: good practice advice*. The download is free and helpful cycling websites are listed on page 79.

Ideally, use the same bike for training as you intend to ride on the route: this should be either a mountain bike or a robust hybrid, not a road bike. Although much of the route is fairly flat, beyond Fort Augustus it contains some stretches with stiff hill climbs. In terms of UK mountain bike trail grading, most of the southern half would be graded green or blue, but north of Fort Augustus there are significant sections of red. If coming from a distance, you may prefer to hire a bike in the Great Glen. Some bike shops offer a pickup service in conjunction with your hire, which simplifies returning the bike.

No-one should undertake the Great Glen Way casually, because the weather in Scotland is so unpredictable. On any given day in the Highlands, you may experience weather typical of any season, and perhaps all four. This adds variety to the experience, but also makes it important to be prepared for anything and to have suitable clothing.

This book has been planned in the recommended direction, going north-east from Fort William to Inverness. The prevailing wind in Scotland is south-westerly, so you are more likely to have the wind at your back. The longest section is your approach to Inverness, by which time you'll be well into your stride. Finally, on average there should be less rain as you move north-east: Inverness has annual rainfall of 25 inches (635 mm), compared with Fort William's 80 (2030 mm). This may be good for morale.

Note on map orientation

To optimise its scale, all our map pages have north rotated by 39° anti-clockwise. Readers using compass and other maps can orientate them easily from our kilometre grid which reminds that magnetic north is at the upper left of each page. The only exceptions are the two town plans (pages 39 and 77) which show north traditionally.

How long will it take?

Most walkers will spread the route over five to seven days, whereas most cyclists will complete it in two to four days. How long you need depends not only on your fitness and attitude, but also on your time available and the pace you find comfortable. Don't underestimate the time you need: allow yourself leisure to enjoy the fine scenery and wildlife viewing opportunities. Read section 2·4 to decide whether you want to build in time for any hill side-trips. These could add anything from half a day to a couple of overnights to the overall duration. Table 1a shows distances and suggested sections for walkers, and Table 1b for cyclists.

Table 1a Six-day itinerary for walkers

		miles	km
3·1	Fort William to Gairlochy Locks	11·0	17·7
3·2	Gairlochy to Laggan Locks	12·3	19·8
3·3*	Laggan Locks to Fort Augustus	11·2	18·0
3·4*	Fort Augustus to Invermoriston	7·3	11·8
3·5	Invermoriston to Drumnadrochit	15·6	25·1
3·6**	Drumnadrochit to Inverness	19·6	31·5
	Total	77·0	123·9

*For a 5-day itinerary, combine sections 3·3 and 3·4.

** For options for splitting section 3·6, see page 7.

Table 1b Three-day itinerary for cyclists

		miles	km
3·1 - 3·3	Fort William to Invergarry	28·1	45·2
3·4 - 3·5	Invergarry to Drumnadrochit	31·2	50·2
3·6	Drumnadrochit to Inverness	19·6	31·6
	Total	78·9	127·0

For a 4-day itinerary, split the middle section.
For a 2-day ride, break the route at Fort Augustus or Invermoriston.

Plan how you will reach the start and return from the finish. Depending on distance, you may need to overnight in Fort William and/or Inverness. Table 2 on page 13 gives estimated times by various forms of travel to help you plan. Depending on distance, you could perhaps walk or ride the Way in sections, for example over a few week-ends, making use of the regular bus service along the A82.

Part 3 describes the Way in six sections, and Table 1a shows distances for each of these. Fast and fit walkers may prefer to combine two sections for a five-day itinerary, and others in less of a hurry may spread it over seven days. Table 1b shows how cyclists may wish to complete the route over three days, with options for two or four days.

Route options include the Invergarry Link route from Laggan Locks to Aberchalder on the western shore of Loch Oich. This adds about 2 miles/3 km to the overall distance but it opens up more choice of accommodation: see pages 10-11. It is fully waymarked and shown in alternative route style on our mapping.

Fingal approaching Kytra Lock

Two sections above Loch Ness known as the High Route were opened in 2014. These create exciting options for walkers to enjoy much better views. The gradients are more challenging and will slightly increase the time you need: see pages 58-60 and 65-6. These new sections are not recommended for cyclists because they contain some very steep parts, and a few obstacles such as stone cross-drains which which would involve dismounting. In terms of UK mountain bike trail grading, they would be graded mainly red with some black parts. The High Route options are waymarked and shown on our mapping and in altitude profiles.

Note that the last section is very long – 20 miles (32 km) – and many, perhaps most, walkers will find that too long for a single day. Dearth of accommodation makes it difficult to split unless you are willing and able to camp at Abriachan. Here are two options to consider:

- Spend two nights at Drumnadrochit (Drum), and walk as far as Blackfold on the first day (12 miles/19 km); some tour operators and B&B hosts will organise a vehicle pickup from Blackfold back to Drum, returning you to Blackfold next morning to complete the route.

- Take a boat-based approach to walking or cycling the whole route, which allows the distance to be split over six full days and two half days, hosted by Caledonian Discovery: see pages 23 and 78.

Read also the sections about the best time of year and accommodation (pages 10-11) before deciding when to go and how long to spend.

South-west from Meall a' Cholumain

Terrain and gradients

The Way passes over a variety of surfaces, mostly firm ones such as canal towpath and railway trackbed, forest tracks and minor roads. In places, however, the going can be rocky, boggy and challenging. Both sections of the High Route climb high above the traditional route, the southern one to 316 m (1040 ft) and the northern to a new high point of 422 m (1385 ft). The constructed paths are in places steep or very steep, but the surface is sound and the views rewarding.

High Route terrain: unsuitable for cyclists

Many people imagine the Way as running along canal towpath, and they tend to underestimate the amount of climbing and descending involved. To complete the traditional Great Glen Way, you gain over 1400 m (4600 ft) of altitude even though you never go higher than 382 m (1250 ft) above sea level. If you use both sections of the High Route, that figure increases considerably.

The altitude profile below shows the overall trend, which is that the gradients become more challenging in the later sections – assuming that you start from Fort William as we recommend. There is a more detailed altitude profile at the head of each section in Part 3: these are worth close study if you are in doubt about whether to split a section, or about how long it will take you to complete.

The route, including the optional sections of Invergarry Link and High Route, is fully waymarked with the 'thistle in a hexagon' logo which appears on pale blue posts and fingerposts and on information boards. Consistent waymarking and generally modest gradients make this route a good choice for your first long-distance route.

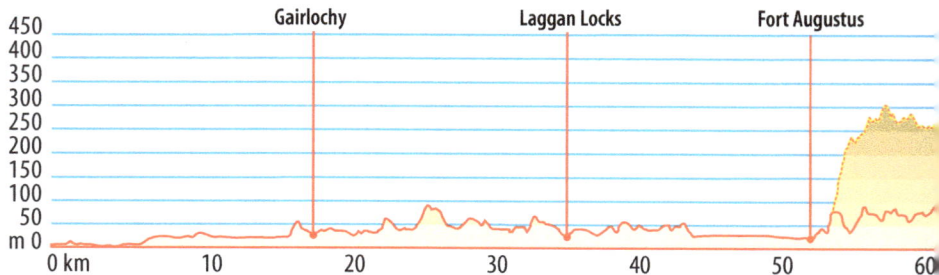

Navigation and waymarking

The photos on this page will help you to recognise them, but it's easy to miss a waymarker if you are distracted. Refer to our maps often, and if you haven't seen a waymarker for 30-40 minutes the chances are that you are off-route – albeit waymarking is sparse on some long straight sections where no options exist. If in doubt, It's often better to backtrack to the last waymarker than to carry on regardless. If you plan to venture off the Way, especially into the mountains, be sure to carry also the largest scale map you can obtain. Follow the Mountain Code: see page 27.

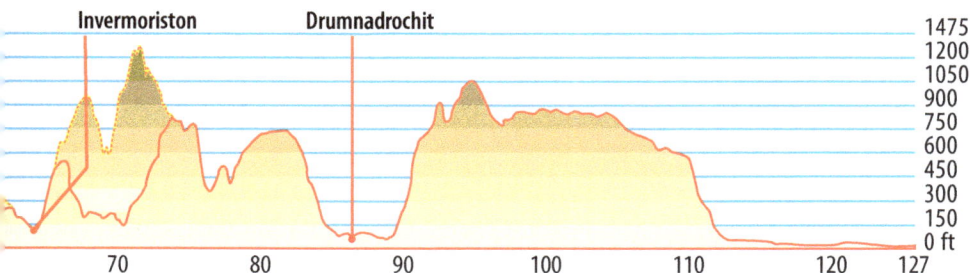

What is the best time of year?

Fortunately for those who have little choice over their holiday dates, there is no bad time of year to walk the Way, albeit winter is unlikely to work well unless you can go at short notice, on a good forecast. Be prepared for cold, wet and windy weather at any time of year and you could be pleasantly surprised. You may be lucky enough to experience sunshine and good visibility. Think about the following:

- At this latitude, winter has short days: hours of daylight vary from 6-7 hours in late December to 17-18 in late June.
- Winter restricts your choice of side-trips; some attractions are open only in season (typically from Easter to October).
- From May to September, expect pests such as midges (small biting insects), ticks and clegs (horse-flies), especially in still weather: see page 79 for useful websites, including one on ticks and Lyme disease.
- On winter timetables, public transport is less frequent: see page 78 for contact details.
- In summer, the area is very popular with visitors and there's heavy pressure on accommodation; however, in winter many B&Bs are closed for the season.

On balance, and if you are free to choose, the ideal months are probably May/June and September/early October. July and August are the busiest times for visitors, with heavy demand for accommodation.

Accommodation and facilities

If completing the Way in a single expedition, the goal is to split the distance into manageable sections that end somewhere with accommodation that suits your budget and is available. Whatever your preference, don't leave accommodation to chance: it can be scarce at any time of year and booking is essential.

Specialist tour operators can organise it all for you, or you can research the options using search engines, VisitScotland or the official Great Glen Way app or website: see page 78. Remember that online listings are never comprehensive when businesses have to pay for inclusion. Consider also searching on Google maps and *airbnb.co.uk*.

The table on page 11 summarises what is available where, or rather what was available in 2019. It's always worth checking online, in case a B&B re-opens in Abriachan, for example, or a campsite has closed since we went to press. The Invergarry Link route runs on the other shore of Loch Oich from the main Way, so overnighting at Invergarry entails going a further 6 miles (10 km) beyond Laggan Locks. Many, especially cyclists, will appreciate the greater flexibility and choice of accommodation that this option offers.

Be aware of long gaps between places with food and drink, and stock up in advance. Many B&Bs will make you a packed lunch given enough notice. Also ask your host in advance if you need an early breakfast or any help with travel arrangements. This applies particularly to walkers who want to split the section from Drum to Inverness at Blackfold: see page 7.

Facilities along the Way

Cheaper than B&Bs, especially for solo walkers, are youth hostels at Fort William (Glen Nevis) and Inverness. People of any age can stay at these, and SYHA membership is optional. There are independent hostels at Fort William, South Laggan, Invergarry, Fort Augustus, Alltsigh, Drumnadrochit and Inverness: see page 78 for contact details for SYHA and Scottish Independent Hostels. Cheaper still, but more strenuous because of the need to carry camping and cooking equipment, are various camping options. Commercial campsites generally have toilets and showers; some have laundries. You'll find them along the Way near Fort William (Glen Nevis), near Gairlochy, Fort Augustus, Drumnadrochit, Abriachan and near Inverness. Details are on the official website.

Scottish Canals has established informal campsites called Trailblazer Rest Sites for the Great Glen Canoe Trail. These are small waterside sites on Loch Lochy (at Glas-dhoire), Loch Oich (Leiterfearn) and at Kytra Lock; there are also two on the south side of Loch Ness. They are available also for walkers and cyclists, but are restricted to small groups with small tents and for single nights only. There are also informal canalside pitches at Moy Bridge, Gairlochy Locks, Aberchalder Bridge, Kytra Lock, Dochgarroch Lock, and at the Seaport Marina, Inverness. There is a seasonal café with camping pods and toilet/shower facilities at Laggan North.

	miles from last place	km from last place	B&B/ hotel	hostel/ bunkhouse	campsite	pub/ café	shop
Fort William			✓	✓	✓	✓	✓
Banavie	4·0	6·4	✓	1	1	✓	1
Gairlochy	6·7	10·8	✓		✓		
Laggan Locks	12·7	20·4	✓	✓		✓	
Invergarry[2]			✓	✓		✓	✓
Aberchalder	5·9	9·5			✓	✓ [3]	
Fort Augustus	4·8	7·7	✓	✓	✓	✓	✓
Invermoriston	8·9	14·3	✓		✓	✓	✓
Alltsigh	4·3	6·9	✓	✓			
Drumnadrochit	10·2	16·4	✓	✓	✓	✓	✓
Abriachan	7·5	12·1			✓	✓	
Inverness	12·5	20·1	✓	✓	✓	✓	✓

1 hostels and shop in Corpach, near Banavie; Linnhe Lochside campsite is 2 miles offroute
2 on the Invergarry Link route, 6 miles/10 km beyond Laggan Locks
3 Thistle Stop, on the A82 between Invergarry and Fort Augustus; seasonal

Use of the Trailblazer composting toilets, and also of the facility blocks (toilets and showers) along the Caledonian Canal, can be hired. In 2019 the cost was £10 per person for the whole route, which covers key rental for access to all facilities. This option is open to walkers and cyclists as well as paddlers. For more information, follow the Trailblazer Rests link from our website *www.rucsacs.com/links/ggw* or phone 01463 725 500.

Under the Scottish Outdoor Access Code (see below) wild camping is generally allowed for small numbers for up to two or three nights in any one place. This is low-impact independent camping without any facilities. If you opt for this, be careful to leave no traces of your campsite. Avoid camping in enclosed fields of crops or farm animals, and keep well away from buildings, roads or historic structures. Take extra care to avoid disturbing deer stalking or grouse shooting. Before camping close to a house or building, seek the owner's permission. On the canal banks, note that camping is prohibited anywhere except in the designated places listed on page 11.

While on the Way, you will need to relieve yourself from time to time. Some walkers and cyclists hire the Scottish Canals key for toilet access alone. Others rely on public toilets where available: Fort William, Corpach, Fort Augustus, Invermoriston, Drumnadrochit, Abriachan forest car park and Inverness. Some public toilets charge for access, others may be located inside other buildings, perhaps labelled "Comfort Partner".

If a toilet is not available, choose a discreet spot at least 50 m away from paths and buildings, preferably further, and as far as possible from any water course. Please bury human waste in a deep hole; people who are wild camping usually carry a light trowel for digging, others may improvise using whatever is to hand.

The Scottish Outdoor Access Code

The Scottish Outdoor Access Code interprets the access rights established by law: see panel below. The Great Glen Way attracts walkers from all over the world, many of them lacking experience of livestock and farming. The countryside provides a livelihood for its residents: please show consideration for them and their livestock. Lambing can occur any time from March to June: never disturb pregnant ewes, nor approach young lambs. Cattle can be fiercely protective of their young, and walkers should give them a wide berth, especially if there are calves around.

Everyone has the right to be on most land and inland water providing they act responsibly. Your access rights and responsibilities are explained fully in the Scottish Outdoor Access Code

KNOW THE CODE BEFORE YOU GO
outdooraccess-scotland.com

Whether you're in the outdoors or managing the outdoors, the key things are to
- **take responsibility for your own actions**
- **respect the interests of other people**
- **care for the environment.**

Find out more by visiting *www.outdooraccess-scotland.com* or by contacting Scottish Natural Heritage; see page 78 for details.

Planning your travel

Once you have considered the route options, whether going on foot or by bike, how long you expect to need to enjoy the Way and where you intend to overnight, you can plan your travel. Consult our maps together with Table 2 below. There are good train and coach services to Fort William via Glasgow and Edinburgh, and also good return connections from Inverness back to Glasgow and Edinburgh. Table 2 shows the fastest scheduled times for bus and train as of 2019. Car journey times are the fastest likely within speed limits, with no allowance for traffic hold-ups and minimal fuel stops. All figures are rough guidelines only. Check schedules in advance, as winter timetables may be restricted: see page 78 for contact details for airlines, buses and trains.

Table 2 Distances and journey times between selected places					
	Approx mile	km	by bus	by train	by car
Glasgow / Fort William	100	160	3h 05m	3h 45m	2h 30m
Edinburgh / Fort William	145	235	4h 15m	4h 50m	3h 30m
Inverness / Fort William	70	110	1h 50m	n/a	1h 45m
Inverness / Glasgow	165	265	2h 05m	3h 20m	3h 30m
Inverness / Edinburgh	160	265	3h 45m	3h 20m	3h 30m
Glasgow / Edinburgh	45	70	1h 05m	46m	1h

Inverness Airport is 10 miles east of the city and has direct flights to several regional airports and to Manchester and London (Heathrow, Gatwick and Luton), as well as (in 2019) Belfast, Dublin and Amsterdam. Budget fares are available on most flights subject to the usual restrictions.

Regular bus services operate along the A82 trunk road through the Great Glen from Fort William to Inverness: during summer there are at least seven services daily. Buses are useful for returning to your starting-point, at least for walkers; bikes are allowed on Citylink buses only if completely covered in a bike bag or box. Some bus companies don't accept dogs, so check in advance if your dog can travel with you.

We make some suggestions for hill and mountain side-trips on pages 27-31. Depending on the season, such plans could add to the amount of clothing and gear that you need to bring. Highland weather cannot be predicted reliably at long range: always check the night before departure.

Dogs

Under SOAC, dogs must be always be kept under close control and on a lead in areas with sheep and lambs. Useful advice is provided in the free leaflet *Dog Owners* published by Scottish Natural Heritage: see page 78. Before deciding to take your dog along the Way, remember that many accommodations do not accept dogs: check before booking.

Your main responsibilities when walking a dog in the countryside are:

Please keep all dogs under close control and on a lead during lambing season (April to June)

- **don't let your dog approach or worry livestock; give lambs, calves and their mothers an especially wide berth**
- **if you can't avoid going into a field with farm animals, keep your dog on a short lead or under close control and keep as far as possible from the animals**
- **if cattle react aggressively and move towards you, keep calm, let the dog go and take the shortest, safest route out of the field**
- **during the bird breeding season (usually April to July), keep your dog on a short lead or under close control in open country and near water**
- **if your dog defecates in a public open place, pick up and remove its mess.**

What to bring

People vary widely in what they need for comfort and whether they expect to carry everything for themselves or to rely on a baggage service. If you are camping, letting a baggage handler deal with your heavy stuff may let you enjoy your walk more. If you are staying in B&Bs or hostels, start by reviewing what you need to walk comfortably each day. If the overnight extras are little more than clean underwear and a toothbrush, you may decide to remain self-reliant.

Baggage handling in the Great Glen is offered by several firms. You can contact them directly, but if using a tour operator to organise your accommodation, you'll find this service included. Contact details are given under *Support services* on our web page ***www.rucsacs.com/books/ggw***.

Think carefully about what to take and do any specialised shopping ahead of time. Once on the Way, shops are scarce. Between Fort William and Fort Augustus, there is only one shop with groceries, a detour from Laggan Bridge. Beyond Invermoriston there is Loch Ness Clay Works at Grotaig – a combined pottery and café generally open daily, but phone 01456 450 402 to check. Drumnadrochit now has a good Scotmid supermarket, but between Drum and Inverness there is only one rustic café on the Way, at Abriachan, with campsite (tel 01463 861 462). Refreshments are also available at Invergarry on the Link route: see page 11.

Packing checklist

The checklist below refers to the daytime needs of a walker. Experienced walkers may differ about what is essential or desirable, but novices may appreciate a starting-point. Normally you will be wearing the first three or four items and carrying the rest in your rucksack. Those who use a baggage transfer service will be tempted to take much more than those who carry for themselves: if you resist this temptation, you will waste much less time unpacking and packing every day.

Cyclists will have different needs, especially for footwear, and may benefit even more from using a baggage transfer service.

Essential

- comfortable, waterproof walking boots
- specialist walking socks
- breathable clothing in layers
- waterproof jacket and over-trousers
- hat and gloves
- water carrier and plenty of water (or purification tablets/drops)
- enough food to last between supply points
- guidebook with maps
- first aid kit including blister treatment
- toiletries and overnight necessities
- insect repellent and sun protection (May to September)
- rucksack (at least 30 litres)
- waterproof rucksack cover or liner, e.g. bin (garbage) bag
- enough cash in pounds sterling: credit cards are not always acceptable and cash machines are sparse along the Way.
- Bin bags have many uses e.g. store wet clothing or prevent hypothermia (cut holes for your head and arms).

Desirable

- compass, map, whistle and torch: essential if you are hill climbing or hiking in winter
- walking pole(s)
- binoculars: useful for spotting wildlife
- camera (ideally light and rugged), also spare batteries, memory card
- pouch or secure pockets, to keep small items handy but safe
- gaiters (to keep mud and water off trouser legs and boots)
- toilet tissue (biodegradable)
- water purification tablets or drops
- spare socks: changing socks at lunchtime can relieve damp feet
- spare shoes (e.g. trainers or trekking sandals)
- small towel
- notebook and pen
- mobile phone (cellphone): useful for arrangements but don't rely on one for emergencies. Reception can be patchy.

For campers

If you are camping, you need much more gear, including tent, sleeping gear, camping stove, fuel, cooking utensils and food. Your rucksack will need to be larger e.g. 50-80 litres, and camping could add 5-10 kg to its weight. Previous experience is advisable.

2·1 Loch Ness and the Great Glen fault

Loch Ness extends over one third of the Great Glen's length and dominates the northern half of the Way, stretching from Fort Augustus to a few miles short of Inverness. It's about 10,000 years old, dating from the end of the last Ice Age when the Great Glen was occupied by a massive glacier. Loch Ness is the centre of an area of outstanding natural beauty, with significant wildlife interest in its waters, around its shores and in its beautiful side glens. This section describes the loch and its famous wildlife, then turns to the formation of the Great Glen fault.

With an average depth of over 600 feet (185 m) and a length of 23 miles (37 km), Loch Ness holds over two cubic miles of water – more than all the lakes and reservoirs in England and Wales put together, and three times as much as Loch Lomond. Draining water from a huge area (700 square miles), it forms one of the largest freshwater systems in Europe. At its deepest point near Urquhart Castle, soundings have recorded over 750 feet (225 m), deeper than most of the North Sea. Its rock bed is covered in thick sediment and clay, so its true depth is even greater than has yet been recorded.

Because of its great depth, the loch has never been known to freeze. It is so massive that it affects the surrounding land climate, where snow seldom lies for very long. Most of its waters never become colder than 5°C even after prolonged sub-zero weather. During the summer months, layers of warmer water lie above the denser colder mass, divided by a region of sharp temperature change called a *thermocline*. The water is still too cold for many living things, and some of its inhabitants are left over from glacial times. The combination of steep contours, wind and waves makes its shores inhospitable.

Loch Ness, Britain's greatest freshwater system

What lives in Loch Ness?

It is Scotland's most famous loch mainly because of persistent reports of sightings of a monster usually known as 'Nessie' Although Loch Morar is even deeper, plumbing depths of over 1000 feet (305 m), its alleged monster Morag has never rivalled Nessie's worldwide fame.

The monster legend dates from 565 AD when St Columba is said to have banished a creature from Loch Ness's northern end. Published reports date from 1868, when the *Inverness Courier* first mentioned the 'tradition of a huge fish gambolling in the loch'. Headlines were made by the 1933 sightings during major works on the A82, when the *Courier* again reported 'a strange spectacle on Loch Ness'.

In 1934 the the monster industry gained impetus from the publication of surgeon R K Wilson's photograph of a serpentine neck rising from a humped body. This infamous hoax was followed by hundreds of fresh photographs and thousands of sightings. Many sincere and frightened eye-witnesses described strange creatures of various shapes and sizes. Various causes have been put forward for these sightings, for example mirages and atmospheric illusions, drifting logs, boat wakes, diving birds, swimming deer, visiting seals, otters' tails and huge migrant fish.

In the 1960s the Loch Ness Investigation Bureau made systematic searches, first on the surface, then underwater, using mini-submarines and sonar. In 1987 Operation Deepscan had 20 motor cruisers sweeping the entire loch with a sonar curtain. Later, the Rosetta Project brought back long columns of sediment collected from the floor. These time capsules show how pollution and radioactivity have reached its depths. The scientific data collected by these investigations is stranger than the monster fiction; it is presented imaginatively by the Loch Ness Centre: see page 68.

Dusk over Loch Ness

Loch Ness is relatively poor in nutrients compared with, for example, Loch Lomond. Although there are occasional migrant seals in pursuit of salmon, the top resident in the Loch Ness food chain is the Ferox trout, a predatory variety of Brown trout. It is a large fish that can grow up to 80 cm (31 in) in length, and can live for up to 23 years. In the collage below it is shown in pursuit of a shoal of six Arctic charr, its favourite food source. The pursuit of charr may take the trout to great depths: charr have been netted from as deep as 220 m/730 ft, the deepest recorded fish catch to date. They are relicts of the Ice Age.

Arctic charr in turn feed directly on plankton - tiny organisms that are vital to the food chain. The creatures shown below at lower centre and right are animal plankton, less than 1 mm long (*Bythotrephes* and *Diaptomus*). Animal plankton feed on even smaller plant plankton such as those shown at upper right (*Tabellaria*) and bottom left (*Asterionella*). Based on analysis of the food chain, scientists have calculated that there simply isn't enough food in the loch to sustain a resident population of large predators, let alone a monster.

Fish and plankton in Loch Ness (not to scale)

The Great Glen fault

Scotland's longest glen is known by three names: the Great Glen, Gleann Mhor (Gaelic for 'big glen') or Glen Albyn. It is unusual in that it leads to open water at both ends, to Loch Linnhe and the Moray Firth. It joins the Atlantic Ocean to the North Sea, making an island of the north-west Highlands.

The glen follows the line of a major geological fault created about 380 million years ago. North-west Scotland was originally joined to parts of Canada, Greenland and northern Norway. Geologists agree that there was a major upheaval about that time, although theories differ about the fault's exact formation. According to W Q Kennedy, the whole land mass sheared off and was shifted 65 miles to the south-west.

In the Ice Age about 20,000 years ago, giant glaciers covered nearly all of Scotland and northern England. The ice was up to a mile thick in places, wiping out plant and animal life, and scouring a wide corridor along the line of the fault. This is still Britain's most seismically active area, with an average of over 60 earthquakes per century (Richter 4).

2·2 The Caledonian Canal

The Great Glen fault is what made the Caledonian Canal possible. Only 22 miles of this historic waterway are man-made; the other 38 rely on the natural waterways of Lochs Lochy, Oich and Ness. The Great Glen Way clings closely to the canal route all the way from Corpach to Fort Augustus. Thereafter it diverges to its north, joining the canal very briefly in the final approach to Inverness.

The canal was first proposed in 1773, and was designed by two engineers, William Jessop and Thomas Telford, with work beginning in 1803. Jessop took on Telford, the son of a Dumfries-shire shepherd, as his assistant and although they worked on it jointly, Telford seems to have been given most of the credit.

It was an ambitious venture, demanding the moving of huge amounts of material and creating work for up to 1200 labourers. Telford and Jessop had proposed a canal depth of 20 feet, but dredging problems restricted it to about 14 feet. It took 19 years to complete, and cost £912,000 - a huge sum of money at the time. There were great celebrations when it finally opened in 1822.

The canal was built mainly to create jobs and boost trade, but commercial use was never great, partly because of its limited depth. It was a lifeline for lochside communities in an era when roads were poor or absent. Later, it provided a safe passage, avoiding the Pentland Firth, for thousands of naval vessels during World War 1. Otherwise leisure craft became its main users. It was paid for entirely by public money, and remains the earliest example of nationalised transport in Britain.

The maximum size of ships that can navigate the canal is 35 foot beam by 150 foot long by 13·5 foot draught (or 160 foot long by 9 foot draught), and the speed limit is six miles per hour (9·7 kph). For contact details for the canal and its operating hours and regulations, see page 78.

Boat passing through Cullochy Lock

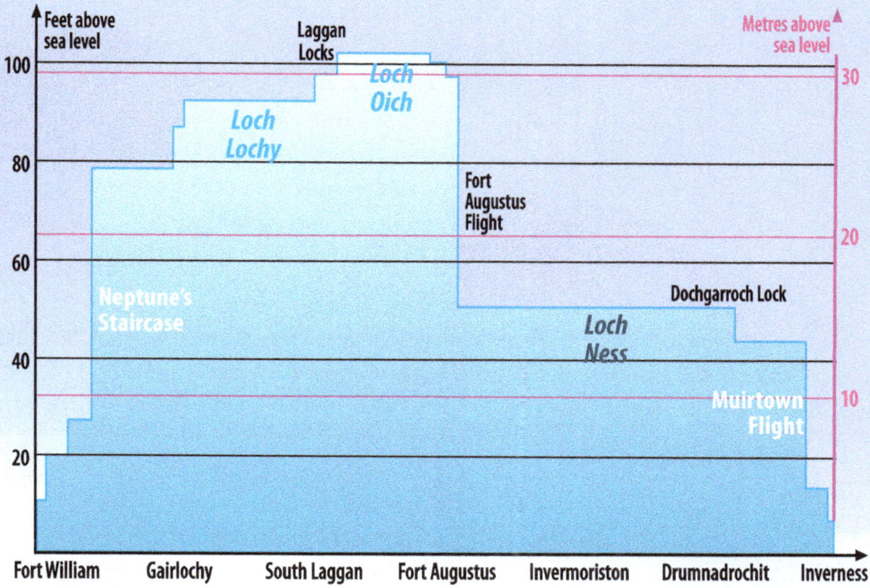
Feet above sea level
Metres above sea level
100
80
60
40
20
30
20
10
Laggan Locks
Loch Oich
Loch Lochy
Fort Augustus Flight
Neptune's Staircase
Dochgarroch Lock
Loch Ness
Muirtown Flight
Fort William
Gairlochy
South Laggan
Fort Augustus
Invermoriston
Drumnadrochit
Inverness

Its highest point is Loch Oich, at 106 feet (32 m) above sea level. Water drains from its southern end towards the Atlantic, and leaves its northern end towards the North Sea. Differences in level between the lochs are handled by 29 locks, each of which raises or lowers the level by up to eight feet. From the towpath, it's fascinating to watch the boats being worked through the locks.

Notice as you walk that after the watershed the lock gates open in the opposite direction. Lock gates are always angled so that the pressure of water at the higher level holds them closed. This is obvious in the photograph of Neptune's Staircase, a flight of eight locks which lifts boats by 64 feet (19·5 m) over only 1500 feet (457 m) horizontal: see page 44.

Originally locks were worked by muscle power and leverage. The lock-keeper slotted a long wooden pole into each of the outward-facing sockets and rotated the capstan to open or close a lock gate. The poles were sometimes stored on top of the capstan in a tall pyramid supported by square sockets set into the top.

Capstans were worked by leverage

Muirtown locks

Although by 1968 all the locks had been mechanised, many of the capstans are still in place on the towpath. There is a good example, complete with poles, in the Canal Visitor Centre in Fort Augustus: see page 55.

The canal has many other interesting features, including ten swing bridges and various weirs, aqueducts and tunnels.

There are distinctive pepper-pot lighthouses at Corpach, Gairlochy, Fort Augustus and Loch Dochfour (Bona). Originally they were occupied and worked by lighthouse-keepers, but later all were automated.

Walking to the sea locks

To see the canal 'end-to-end', it's worth extending your walk to visit both sea locks. To reach Corpach lighthouse from Fort William is a short diversion from the Way: see page 42.

At the Inverness end, the sea lock is 1·7 miles (2·7 km) from the end of the Way at Inverness Castle. To reach the canal at Muirtown Bridge by a simple route (not the best, but easy to navigate), cross the River Ness just north of the castle. Turn third right at the traffic lights up Kenneth Street, which becomes Telford Street. Follow it to reach the bridge across the canal: the Muirtown flight of four locks is to your left and the boat basin to your right. See the plan on page 76.

Muirtown Basin once served as a second harbour to Inverness, but after ships became larger, its use declined. On its west side there's a wall plaque that celebrates Telford's achievement with a poem written by his friend Robert Southey, then Poet Laureate, to celebrate the canal's opening.

Corpach sea lock with lighthouse

Clachnaharry sea lock

Follow the towpath along the west side of Muirtown Basin. To reach Clachnaharry sea lock, you must cross the railway line – it's unsupervised, so take care – then walk out to the small beacon. The sea lock was built out into the water because of shoals in the Beauly Firth, and it affords great views of the Firth (look out for dolphins and seals) and Ben Wyvis to the north-west. Cross the canal by any lock gate to return to Muirtown Bridge along the east side of the basin.

The Caledonian Discovery option

Caledonian Discovery has been offering their own week-long version of the route since before the Great Glen Way opened in 2002. Their *Walk the Great Glen* itinerary (which can also be cycled) follows the Way closely for most of its length, but runs between Banavie and Clachnaharry sea locks. The barge moves while its guests walk or cycle, allowing the distance to be split comfortably over five full days and two part days. They also offer options to canoe the Great Glen or to bike it in a 3-night cruise.

The company operates two Dutch barges, Fingal and Ros Crana, which accommodate 12 guests each, and which also carry bikes, canoes and other equipment. Because you sleep onboard, you never have to carry more stuff than you need for the day, and the deal includes all meals and a guide when ashore. See page 78 for contact details.

Fingal motoring along Laggan Avenue

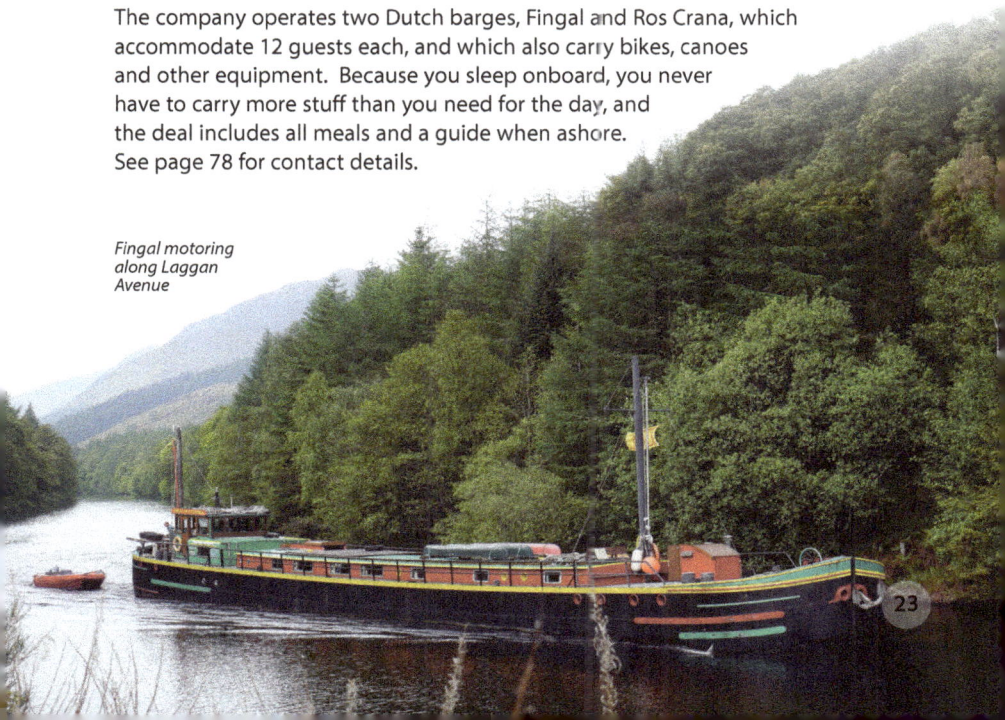

2·3 Historical background

Hill forts of the Great Glen

Ten hilltop forts testify to the Great Glen's strategic importance since the Iron Age. They may also have been used as a line-of-sight signalling system using beacons. The most accessible to Great Glen users are Torr Dhuin (from Fort Augustus) and Craig Phadrig (from Inverness). Dun Deardail is a small diversion off the West Highland Way to the south of Fort William, not to be confused with Dun Dearduil at Farigaig, near Foyers on the south shore of Loch Ness. The forts are worth visiting for the glorious views from their hilltop sites. Nearly all are owned by the Forestry and Land Scotland (FLS): for more information, visit its website *forestryandland.gov.scot*.

Some of these forts are called *vitrified* (glassy) because of the shiny appearance of their stones after intense fires had partly melted them. Mystery surrounds the cause of these fires, whether deliberate or accidental, but they must have burned for long periods at extremely high temperatures.

Torr Dhuin stands above Kytra Loch and can be reached by an excellent FLS waymarked path in under an hour from the car park at Auchterawe, about two miles/3 km south of Fort Augustus. From the Way, follow signs for River Oich Forest Walks to reach the car park. The fort gives excellent views over the canal and towards the Corrieyairack Pass.

A walk to Craig Phadrig

For a clearer view of a hill fort, we recommend Craig Phadrig ('Patrick's hill'), a large oval structure sitting atop a splendid wooded crag at the south- western edge of Inverness. You could walk there in 50-60 minutes from Muirtown Bridge: see map page 76. Alternatively, bus no 3 (signed Craig Dunain) goes from Queensgate in the city centre to the Balnafettack Road stop. Walk up Leachkin Brae (pronounced *larkin bray*). From the car park, follow instructions on page 25 from paragraph two. Allow 30-45 minutes for the Hill Fort Trail walk (1·2 miles/1·9 km).

If walking from central Inverness, head west along Telford Street and cross Muirtown Bridge, then Canal Road. Turn left up King Brude Road. Follow it for about 1 km, then turn right at traffic lights (Leachkin Road). After 500 m, go straight over the roundabout, then turn second right up Leachkin Brae, signposted for Craig Phadrig.

At the car park, there's an information board with a map showing two waymarked trails. Follow the blue-and-yellow Hill Fort Trail (1·9 km) around a bend and up to a junction where you turn right.

At the next junction turn right, then at the next junction that you reach turn left, still following blue-and-yellow markers. Follow the path up and around the base of Craig Phadrig itself, keeping right and following blue markers where the path bends right.

Where the path starts to descend you'll find an information board. Shortly, an informal path on the right leads up to the summit. A wide gap in the trees gives magnificent views north-westwards

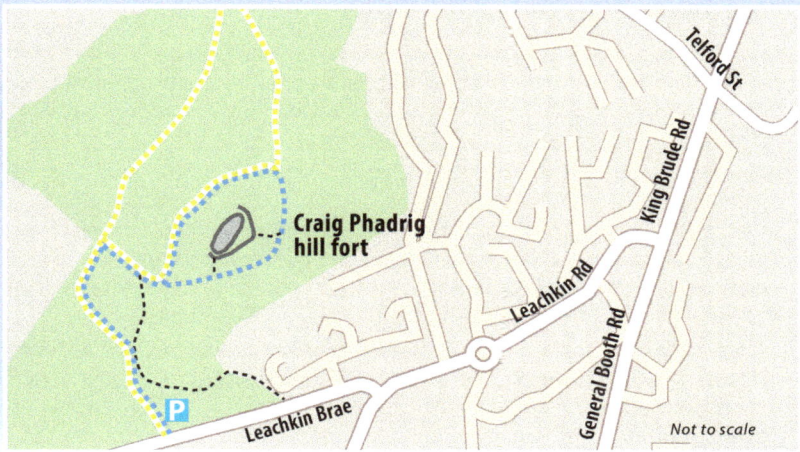

Return to the main path (blue markers) and continue down. At a junction, turn left (blue-and-yellow markers) and left again to return to the start. The fort is thickly covered with grass, but in winter and spring you can clearly see the two concentric oval ramparts, made of stones that once were interlaced with timber and vitrified (glassy) in places. Stones still protrude in places and there's a vitrified section of inner rampart near a pine tree at its northern end. Originally the walls would have been massive – at least 26 feet high and 21 feet thick (8 m high by 6 m thick).

Radioactive carbon dating suggests that it was constructed around 350 BC. Although repeatedly damaged by fire, the site was occupied from time to time for many centuries and became a capital of the Pictish kings.

At the time of St Columba's missionary visit in 580 AD, the pagan King Brude refused him entry. According to legend, the gates mysteriously fell open when Columba knocked, and King Brude and his people were so impressed that they converted to Christianity. This hill was probably the site of the first settlement that later became Inverness.

North-west from Craig Phadrig, with Ben Wyvis distant

25

The Jacobite risings and military roads

In 1688, James VII of Scotland (who was also James II of England) was deposed by popular demand, partly because he was thought to be promoting the Catholic Church. Parliament chose instead his daughter Mary, also of the house of Stewart, who had married the Dutch Protestant William of Orange.

After William and Mary came to the British throne (1688-9), those who supported the other Stewart line of James VII and his son James (the 'Old Pretender') became known as Jacobites: *Jacobus* is Latin for James. Queen Mary showed little interest in Scotland and her Dutch husband, William of Orange, was resented as a foreigner. The unpopularity of the 1707 Act of Union, together with the sense of distance from decisions made in London, gave the Jacobite cause a nationalist flavour.

During 1689-1745, contact was kept up between Scotland and the Jacobite court, first in France then Italy. Two famous Jacobite risings took place in 1715 and 1745. The 'Fifteen' focused on the Old Pretender, and the 'Forty-five' on his son, Charles Edward Stewart, also known as 'Bonnie Prince Charlie' or the 'Young Pretender'.

In 1746, the Battle of Culloden marked the final defeat of the Jacobites. Against advice, Bonnie Prince Charlie insisted on pitched battle on an open site unsuited to his Highlanders' tactics. His army was hungry, sleepless and heavily outnumbered, and government troops routed them in under an hour. About 2000 Jacobites were killed in this battle, the last fought on British soil.

However, 'Bonnie Prince Charlie' remained in Scotland for another five months, living in hiding, being pursued all over the Highlands and islands by the military. Famous among those who protected and helped him at this time is Flora Macdonald, whose statue stands outside Inverness Castle.

Post-Culloden, it became a government priority to make troop movement around the Highlands easier. Barracks were built at Fort William, Fort Augustus and Fort George, and a network of military roads and bridges constructed. Between 1724 and 1740, building was led by General George Wade, an Irishman who served as Commander-in-Chief of the army in North Britain (Scotland). Many of the works credited to Wade were actually built by his deputy William Caulfeild, who was in charge from 1740-67.

Wade built 240 miles of military roads including the Corrieyairack Road from Fort Augustus to Laggan (1731). This rises to 770 m (2500 feet) and for over a century it was the highest maintained public road in Britain. To reach it from Fort Augustus, follow the directions on page 30.

FLORA
MACDONALD

2·4 Hill and mountain side-trips

On pages 28 to 31 we describe four hill climbs as possible side-trips, two from Fort William, one from Fort Augustus and one from Grotaig. The Fort William options include Ben Nevis, the highest peak in Britain, but this is a serious mountain and you need an extra day as well as good luck with the weather. In case you lack either of these, we include also Cow Hill which gives great views of 'the Ben' and can be tackled even in doubtful conditions.

Our next suggestion is Meall a' Cholumain, a small hill above Fort Augustus, your half-way point and a fine place to take time out. Although it's only 315 m (1030 ft), it offers splendid views in return for a modest effort, with historical interest en route.

From Grotaig, you could climb Meall Fuar-mhonaidh (699 m/2293 ft), which on a clear day gives sensational views from the Atlantic to the North Sea. The Way passes through Grotaig and you are then only 420 m in altitude below its summit. The downside is that you are already committed to walking 14·5 miles (23 km) from Invermoriston to Drumnadrochit, and if you are carrying a heavy pack, this side-trip would make it a long, strenuous day. Read the description on page 31, and be prepared to turn back if conditions are poor.

Those who are keen to climb Munros (Scottish mountains whose summit lies over 3000 ft/914 m) may wish to take a day off the Great Glen Way to climb the two above Loch Lochy – Sron a' Choire Ghairbh (935 m) and Meall na Teanga (917 m). Start from the high track half a mile south-west of Kilfinnan, where a sign points to 'Tomdoun (Cam Bhealach)'. After walking 3 miles south-west, parallel to Loch Lochy, strike west to follow the Allt Glas Dhoire upstream to the summit of the pass (bealach). From here, you can climb either Munro, or both in turn. Follow the Mountain Code and take a detailed map.

To report an accident in the Great Glen, telephone 999 or 112.
Be ready to state your location, details of the injury/accident and your contact phone number.

Mountain Code

Before you go
Learn to use a compass and map.
Know the weather signs and local forecast.
Plan within your abilities.
Know simple first aid and the symptoms of exposure.
Know the mountain distress signals.

When you go
Avoid going alone if possible.
Leave a note of your route, and report on your return.
Take windproofs, waterproofs and survival bag.
Take suitable map and compass, torch, water and food.
Wear suitable boots.
Keep alert all day.

In winter
(November to March)
Each person needs an ice-axe and crampons, and to know how to use them.
Learn to recognise dangerous snow slopes.
Group members may need protection, such as climbing rope and technical gear.

Summit cairn on Meall Fuar-mhonaidh

West over Fort William from Cow Hill

Cow Hill (287 m / 942 ft)

time	**from 1½ to 3 hours, depending on start point, time at summit and whether you extend the walk to complete the full circuit (4 miles/6·5 km)**
terrain	**good surface throughout**

Refer to the plan on page 39: from the town centre, pick up the signposted circuit path from the top of Kennedy Road, soon turning right (south-west). Alternatively, from the roundabout bear left up Lundavra Road until it ends at a cattle grid, then turn left through a gate. The two paths merge about 600 m east of Lundavra Road, and you walk uphill for 1 km on open hillside, soon seeing the rounded massif of Ben Nevis.

At a well-marked path junction, turn left for Cow Hill Summit (1·6 km). The views of the Ben improve further, and the track undulates before its final climb to the hilltop mast. At a gate, a sign explains why Highland cattle have been reintroduced and also warns that 'cattle can sometimes take a dislike to dogs'. If walking with a dog, think twice before proceeding and read the advice on page 14.

Highland cattle roam on Cow Hill

From the summit, the panorama is spectacular, with views over Fort William, Lochs Linnhe and Eil and the Caledonian Canal and River Lochy. On a clear day you can follow the line of the Great Glen and its mountains north-east all the way to the distinctive hump of Meall Fear-mhonaidh above Loch Ness.

Return to the path junction and either turn right to retrace your steps or turn left along the Peat Track (signposted for Glen Nevis) to complete the 4-mile circuit.

Ben Nevis (1344m / 4406 ft)

time	**5 to 7½ hours depending on your fitness**
terrain	**well surfaced path (former pony track)**

Before committing yourself to 'The Ben', review your fitness, experience and the weather forecast. Be aware of the dangers posed by poor visibility on the summit plateau (see panel) and be prepared to turn back if need be. Take extra warm clothing and food in addition to your standard walking gear and waterproofs. There are 261 gales each year, on average, with more than 157 inches (4000 mm) of precipitation on the summit and it can snow and hail even in summer. Take a compass and large-scale map (Harvey's 1:25,000 is ideal) and if you don't know how to use them, go with somebody who does. Check the Mountaineering Scotland website for more information: see page 79.

The zigzag pony track was built to service the observatory that worked on the summit from 1883-1904. Please stick closely to its line: taking short-cuts leads to erosion and can disturb ground-nesting birds.

Start from Achintee Farm, 2 km south-east of Fort William. Alternatively, follow the West Highland Way to the Ben Nevis Visitor Centre and cross River Nevis by footbridge. The track steadily climbs the lower shoulder of Meall an t-Suidhe (711 m) for about a mile before the track from Glen Nevis youth hostel joins it from the right. From here on, the gradient increases as it curves anticlockwise around the shoulder and approaches Lochan Meall an t-Suidhe at the col.

Turn sharply south at the track junction and cross the Red Burn in a deep gully: at 675 m you have reached the half-way point, a good place to review progress and conditions. If all is well, continue up the long series of steep zigzags to reach the lunar landscape of the summit plateau. Take care over the descent and read the warning panel.

> ⚠️ *Sadly, people still die on the Ben, caught by worsening weather and confusion on the summit cliffs. If you have any doubts at the halfway point (Red Burn Ford), turn back. In bad weather, the only safe escape route is to walk from the summit cairn 150 metres along a grid bearing of 231°, then follow 282° to clear the plateau. This is marked by tall stone cairns, but you should be competent with a compass to tackle this mountain.*

West over Loch Eil from the Ben's summit

Meall a' Cholumain (315 m / 1033 ft)

time **3-3½ hours from the village centre (12 km) or 2-2½ hours from the minor road**
terrain **sound surfaces**

From Fort Augustus, walk south-west beside the A82; at the caravan park cross to follow the sign 'Cill Chuimein burial ground' along the minor road. Enter the main Kilchuiman burial ground through the gate. It has several graves with literary connections, and many soldiers who died in World War I. Cross the burial ground diagonally, with the footpath sign, to the far corner wall. Climb it by the protruding stone steps.

Follow the track for about 700 m to a minor public road; turn right as signed for the Corrieyairack Pass. Walk along the road for 500 m then turn left with another sign to the pass. Walk up the path for about 75 m to a gate. The sign warns against damage to Wade's Road, a scheduled ancient monument: see page 26 for background. Continue up the grassy track which shortly narrows to a path, then widens again at the entrance to Culachy Farm.

Follow the wide road built for the construction of the Beauly-Denny power line. Continue straight on where the road diverges to the right after about 500 m. Go through the gate in a deer fence and on up to a saddle. Turn off here along a lesser vehicle track towards the hilltop mast and adjacent installations that mark your destination. The track steepens from the ruinous cottage and shed at Knollbuck. Here, at a junction bear left, passing under the power lines.

The mast stands on a flat hilltop, with a marvellous view north-east up Loch Ness, with Meall Fuar-mhonaidh dominating the skyline: see photo below. The Corrieyairack Pass is to the south-east, marked by pylons and a black dot on the skyline.

For an even better view, continue south-west for about five minutes across the peat and heather. Below lies charming Loch Oich, beyond it the broader expanse of Loch Lochy, with Loch Linnhe in the distance: see photo on page 7. Retrace your steps to the minor road and return to Fort Augustus.

North-east over Loch Ness

Meall Fuar-mhonaidh (699 m /2293 feet)

time	**3½ hours round trip**
terrain	**well-defined path but boggy, sometimes very boggy, especially during or after heavy rain**

To climb Meall Fuar-mhonaidh, pronounced meowl fur-vannie, diverge from the Way near Grotaig car park: see page 64, bullet 4. Instead of following the Way right along a road, turn left briefly to a track on the right signposted 'Hill Path' and go through the gate. The path runs between Grotaig Burn and a fence, through mixed woodland rich in bird life. The going can be boggy in places, but some sections have been improved by boardwalk. Follow waymarkers and pass through several gates.

An abrupt change of vegetation confirms that the climb begins in earnest, as you emerge onto open heather-clad hillside. At first it ascends gently, then swings north to climb more steeply. The path, rough and boggy in places, rises steeply to a tall stile over a deer fence. Deer stalking takes place in this area from August to February, so keep to the main path.

Ascend through increasingly exposed moorland, across peat bog and some rocky ground, the gradient varying from gentle to fairly steep. You walk along a low, rounded ridge, with great views over Loch Ness to your left and the hills and moorland to your right. The path is always well-defined, albeit sometimes braided where people have taken different routes to avoid the boggiest bits.

The final half-hour's climb is heralded by a dip in the path, often with some very wet ground. The first cairn you reach is a false summit: just beyond, there's a wonderful view south-west over Lochs Lochy and Oich. Continue west for a further 10 minutes to reach the true summit cairn, the highest of four on the summit plateau, shown on page 27.

On a clear day, you can see all the way from Loch Linnhe beyond Fort William to the Moray Firth beyond Inverness. You see how the Great Glen cuts a swathe through the Highlands, from the Atlantic Ocean to the North Sea. Retrace your steps to Grotaig.

Meall Fuar-mhonaidh from the Way

Oystercatcher

The Great Glen Way runs through three main types of habitat, described below:
• **water-side** • **woodland** • **heath and moorland**.

If you are really keen to spot wildlife, carry binoculars and walk alone, or seek fellow-travellers who share your interest and are willing to keep quiet when it matters. Try to set off soon after sunrise, or go for a stroll in the evening. Animals are much more active at these times than in the middle of the day. Since this applies to midges too, protect your skin thoroughly, especially from May to September and in still weather.

Water-side

Much of the Way lies near water, along man-made canal and the rivers and lochs. Look out for insects, birds and perhaps some small mammals.

Near Corpach, look for oystercatchers in the fields. Their strong orange bills are good at cracking open cockles and mussels, and they are easy to spot. When in flight, their wings show an obvious white-on-black M-shape, and their piercing cries are unmistakeable.

Look out for grey heron hunting for fish and frogs: sometimes they stand tall and motionless in the shallows, at other times they stalk their prey. In flight, they trail their legs and their huge grey wings beat very slowly.

Grey heron hunting

Kestrel

You are likely to see Britain's most widespread bird of prey, the kestrel. It feeds on small mammals, mainly field voles and mice: its excellent eyesight lets it detect their tiny movements in the grass, and it hunts in a fast dive with half-closed wings. Recognise it by its ability to hover and its pointed chestnut-coloured wings.

Because the Great Glen is open to the sea at both ends, some sea birds use it as a corridor. You may see wandering seabirds such as kittiwakes, guillemots, fulmars and shearwaters in the heart of the glen. Look for cormorants hanging out their wings to dry, especially at Invermoriston pier. For wildlife in Loch Ness, see page 17; keep a look-out for anything unexpected on or in the water.

If you are very lucky, you might see the magnificent osprey plunging to the water to carry off a fish in its talons, torpedo-style. Rescued from extinction in Britain, the osprey population has slowly grown in the Highlands since the first pair returned to Loch Garten in 1955. They are visitors, over-wintering in West Africa and returning each spring, often to the same nesting site.

Osprey carrying its prey

33

Woodland

Crested tit perched on Scots pine

The Great Glen is extensively wooded, with a mixture of native species (broad-leaved and pine) and conifers. The productive forests are dominated by non-native species, e.g. Douglas fir, Norway spruce, lodgepole pine and larch (European, Japanese and hybrid).

Forestry and Land Scotland (FLS) owns most of the forest that you pass through, and large areas of their forests have recently reached readiness for felling. Whilst clear felling always looks stark at first, it is the productive use of land that allows the FLS not only to welcome walkers and cyclists, but also to invest in major improvements to the Great Glen Way.

Nowadays, modern forestry policies make for more diversity – not only in species planted, but also in the age structure of the tree population. This means that clear felling can sometimes be avoided. The FLS target is to plant two trees for every one felled, and to retain 20% as open space in newly planted areas. These policies are aimed at supporting all the wildlife niches in a sustainable way.

Birch thrives on higher ground, along with Scots pine and other hardy species. Juniper flourishes on peaty ground, usually in pinewoods, either as a low, spreading variety or as a taller, grey-green bushy shrub up to 1·5 m high. It has pointed leaves and small, hard 'berries' (seed cones). They ripen slowly, becoming blue-black then black, and are used to flavour gin.

Woodland provides food and shelter for wildlife. Tall conifers are important nesting sites for large birds such as ospreys, buzzards and red kites. Native pinewoods support many rare birds, including crested tits, Scottish crossbills and siskins.

Two species of deer are native to Scotland. On high and open ground you may see red deer, often from afar and on the skyline. In summer they move to high ground to escape from pests, whereas in winter they retreat lower for better grazing. In woodland, their smaller cousins the roe deer are more common and have distinctive white rumps, often seen receding into the distance after they have heard your approach.

Red squirrel

Forests are also home to Britain's only native squirrel species, the red squirrel. This lovely woodland mammal is endangered by disease and competition from its American cousin, the grey squirrel. There's a project to save Scotland's red squirrels, so please report sightings on its website: *www.scottishsquirrels.org.uk*.

The pine marten is another charming native mammal. It had become almost extinct in Britain and has protected status. Recently its numbers have increased strongly in many parts of Scotland, including the Great Glen. It is the only predator fast enough to catch squirrels, but recent research shows that it very seldom preys on red squirrels, which are smaller and more agile than greys. By feasting on grey squirrels, the pine marten thus help the reds to recover lost ground – one endangered species helping another.

Pine marten

Buzzard feeding on rabbit

The Way is low-lying between Fort William and Fort Augustus, but rises high above Loch Ness in its north-eastern half: see the profile on pages 8-9. Here you will go through heathery moorland, especially if you choose the High Route – it stays well above the Low Route for a total of over ten miles (16 km).

Scots pine is the iconic moorland tree. After the Ice Age, 8 to 10 thousand years ago, Scots pine re-colonised the Great Glen. It is the only pine tree native to Britain, and like many tall trees it can act as a perch or nesting site for a bird of prey, such as kestrel, peregrine falcon, buzzard, osprey or even red kite.

Buzzards are large birds with a wingspan of 4 ft (1·2 m). They often hold their rounded

Barn owl

wings in a shallow vee when gliding and soaring. They are also known as 'the tourist's eagle', because visitors easily mistake them for eagles. However the buzzard's plaintive mewing call is unmistakable. Moreover, the golden eagle's wingspan is is 6-7·5 ft (1·8-2·3 m), nearly double that of the buzzard. It is found only in remote areas, and at a distance its sihouette resembles a plank of wood in flight – very different from a buzzard.

36

If you see pathways of nibbled heather and blaeberry, look for mountain hare, which are brown but turn white in winter. Compared with brown hare, the mountain hare has shorter ears and its tail lacks a black tip. Hare predators include the fox and golden eagle.

Skylarks have suffered badly on farmland elsewhere, but they flourish in the Great Glen, especially on higher ground. Owls are birds of prey, and (except for short-eared owl) mainly nocturnal. Field voles live on grass, plants and fruit, and comprise up to 90% of the barn owl's diet.

Heather moorland is also home to game birds, notably grouse. Watch and listen for two kinds of grouse: 'red grouse' are actually red-brown, and have plump bodies. The male has distinctive red

Mountain hare

wattles over his eyes. When disturbed, they fly off in a flurry making a call that sounds like 'ge-back. ge-back'. Loss of habitat means their populations are declining.

Black grouse are even rarer than red. Only the male looks black, whereas females are grey-brown and smaller. Males congregate in a mating display known as a lek (gathering) where they fan their lyre-shaped tail and parade their white under-feathers. There's a good chance you may sight black grouse on the Way north-east of Invermoriston, especially if you take the High Route.

Black grouse (male) calling

Fort William

Fort William is the self-styled 'outdoor capital of Scotland' and a regional centre for tourism and shopping. It enjoys a splendid situation as the elbow of two arms of the sea – Loch Linnhe and Loch Eil. It adjoins beautiful Glen Nevis and has as its backdrop Ben Nevis, Britain's highest mountain. It is a Mecca for walkers, climbers, cyclists and other adventure sports enthusiasts.

Glen Nevis offers superb hiking, with its waterfalls, a precarious three-string bridge and a wealth of wild flowers and birds. The Ben Nevis Visitor Centre is open daily year-round (tel 01397 705 922). It provides a variety of information, including about climbing Ben Nevis: see page 29.

The West Highland Museum has information about the town and its fortifications. It's open year-round Monday to Saturday, also on Sunday afternoons in July/August (*www.westhighlandmuseum.org.uk*, tel 01397 702 169). The High Street is the terminus of the West Highland Way, and has a Visitor Information Centre (open daily year-round) and a range of outdoor shops.

Cruise Loch Linnhe to see porpoises, seals and more. In season, several sailings leave daily from the Town Pier: *www.crannog.net/cruises* (tel 01397 700 714). At low tide, more seals will be basking. Two miles north-east on the A82, the Ben Nevis Distillery has a visitor centre and offers tours and tastings. It's open on weekdays year-round, and also at weekends in high season: *www.bennevisdistillery.com* (tel 01397 700 200).

The town's original fort was a crude timber structure built in 1654-5 under Cromwell's command. In 1690 it was replaced by a stone garrison for 1000 soldiers built on the orders of William III (William of Orange). Originally known as 'Inverlochy' (mouth of the Lochy), the place has been called Fort William ever since.

The fort withstood many conflicts, but latterly it fell into disuse. In 1889 the land was bought by the West Highland Railway Company, which built its railway over part of the fort. Its grassed remains are the starting-point of the Way: see page 40.

East from Corpach to Ben Nevis

Treasures of the Earth ☆

Corpach

Banavie

Neptune's
Staircase

Corpach Station ●

🚻

Banavie
Station ●

Caledonian Canal

Lighthouse

A830

Caol

Great Glen Way

A82

River Lochy

Old
Inverlochy
Castle

Ben Nevis
Distillery

Old Fort
(ruins)

🚻

North Road

Station

Belford Road

West Highland Way

River Nevis

Town Pier
(for Seal
Island)

High Street

☆ 🚻
West Highland
Museum

Kennedy Road

Cow Hill
942 ft 287m ▲

Achintee
Farm ■

A82

Ben Nevis
Visitor Centre ☆

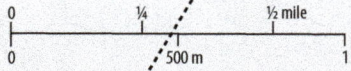

Lundavra Road

N

0   ¼   ½ mile
0   500 m   1 km

39

3·1 Fort William to Gairlochy

Distance	**11·0 miles 17·7 km**
Terrain	**pavement at first, then riverside path, pavement, shoreside path, then canal towpath**
Food and drink	**Fort William (wide range), Caol, Banavie**
Side trips	**Old Inverlochy Castle, Corpach sea lock**
Summary	**easy section, enlivened by mountain views and interesting features including Neptune's Staircase, two aqueducts and canal heritage**

mile 0 — Fort William — 4·3 / 6·9 — Banavie — 4·2 / 6·8 — Loy Aqueduct — 2·5 / 4·0 — 11·0 Gairlochy

- From the railway station turn right to cross the supermarket car park. Then cross the divided road beyond to reach a Great Glen Way fingerpost.

- Follow its left arm ('Terminus') to visit the Old Fort, which has several information boards explaining its history, as well as the Great Glen Way marker stone. Descend through the archway to the right and walk around the perimeter for great views of the old walls, of Loch Linnhe and of the town.

- From the fort, return to the fingerpost to follow its right arm which points past the Underwater Centre and across the An Aird roundabout.

- Continue ahead on cycleway 78 to the left of McDonalds, passing this Welcome sign. Go beside modern housing, and thread your way through another housing estate to a fingerpost pointing across a bridge.

- Cross the River Nevis and on its far side, turn left on a constructed path – embanked to protect it from flooding.

Loch Linnhe from below the Old Fort

Muirshearlich

7

Allt Sheangain

Aqueduct ☆ Torcastle

Caledonian Canal

6

Meall Bhanabhie
327 ▲

Allt Achadh na Dalach

Torlundy

Loch nam
Marag

River Lundy

River Lochy

A82

Allt Mòr

5

Neptune's
Staircase

Banavie

A830

Old
Inverlochy
Castle

Corpach

B8006

Caol

Loch Eil

2

1

A82

N

River Nevis

Camusnagaul

Loch Linnhe

Old
Fort

0

Fort William

i

Cow Hill
287

Old Inverlochy Castle, Ben Nevis distant

- The path runs beside the River Lochy, soon emerging from the trees to give fine views of Ben Nevis and Cow Hill.

- Turn left along a minor road, then cross Soldiers' Bridge (mile 1·4) with views of old Inverlochy Castle. Cyclists should dismount to cross this timber bridge.

- On its far side, turn left (Kilmallie Road) and left into Glenmallie Road to reach Caol's foreshore reserve. The Way turns right, running beside the shore, with good views of Loch Linnhe to your left and Ben Nevis behind you.

Old Inverlochy Castle

This is one of Scotland's earliest stone castles, built in 1260 by Sir John 'the Black' Comyn on a site that had been fortified since AD 273. The castle was built as a square with 9-foot thick walls and a round tower at each corner. It is cared for by Historic Environment Scotland and open daily year-round.

- Continue ahead and go up an incline to reach the Caledonian Canal at Corpach locks. The Way turns right here, but Corpach sea lock is just to the left. Those who enjoy coast-to-coast rituals may wish to dip their boots in the water here.

Pepperpot lighthouse at Corpach

B8005

13

12

Stronaba

Allt Coire Choille-rais

B8004

River Spean

Gairlochy

11

Brackletter

Kilmonivaig

Atllt Coire Chraoibhe

10

Moy Bridge

River Lochy

Cruim Leacainn
232

9

Caledonian Canal

River Loy

Aqueduct

Strone

B8004

8

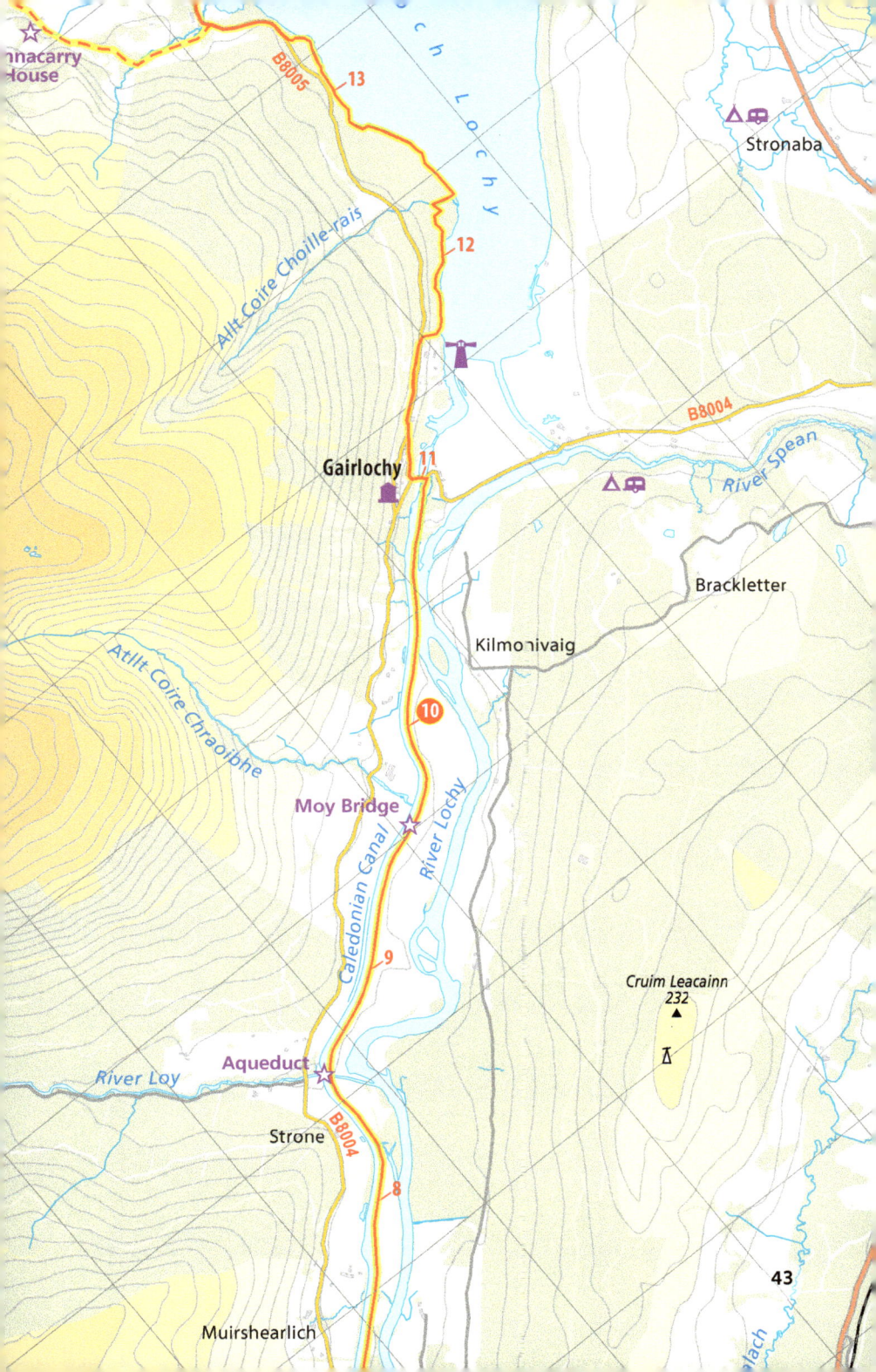

nnacarry
House

Muirshearlich

- The towpath heads north-east to Banavie (pronounced **ban**-a-vee) station, making a right-left dogleg to cross both railway and the A830 road. It then turns right beside Neptune's Staircase, a flight of eight locks.

- Leaving housing behind, still with the canal to its left, the Way now heads through open countryside, with good views across to the Nevis Range.

- The scenery becomes increasingly rural, with some interesting canal features. At mile 6·4, look out for the crossing of the Allt Sheangain where a short detour down to the right lets you see the strong arched structure that carries the canal above the river.

- At mile 8·5 you will see Loy sluices, where a further short detour would let you descend to view the Glen Loy aqueduct. This takes the canal safely above the River Loy, which would otherwise have flooded it. Its main arch

Neptune's Staircase

contained the river, and side arches were for farm traffic. However, the access here can be awash.

- At mile 9·6 you reach the cast iron swing bridge at Moy, the only surviving example of the original design, built in 1822 for the farmer whose land was cut in two by the canal. Each half has to be opened separately, with the bridge-keeper rowing across to open the other half. Scottish Canals has scheduled upgrade work on it for 2020.

- From Moy, it's 1·4 miles/2·2 km to the bridge at Gairlochy, with pleasant views of the River Lochy to your right. Gairlochy is a tiny village with several B&Bs and a campsite nearby. Further services are in Spean Bridge, 4 miles (6·5 km) away by road (B8004 and A82).

Moy Bridge

3·2 Gairlochy to Laggan Locks

Distance 12·3 miles 19·8 km
Terrain a mixture of tarmac and forest paths and tracks
Food and drink Laggan Locks (Eagle Barge)
Side-trip Clan Cameron Museum (Achnacarry), Chia-aig waterfall
Summary fairly easy section along the length of Loch Lochy, with splendid views; Invergarry Link route diverges near the end

```
11·0        4·4              4·6              3·3      23·3
        7·1             7·4              5·3
Gairlochy      Clunes                Glas-dhoire        Laggan Locks
```

This section passes through land owned by the Camerons of Lochiel. Two miles after Gairlochy, there is the option of a diversion to the Clan Cameron Museum at Achnacarry. The first Achnacarry House was built c1655 by the Camerons, but it was destroyed in 1746 to punish them for their role in the Jacobite rising. After rebuilding in1802, it was damaged by fire in World War 2. From 1942-45, it was the base for the arduous training of 25,000 British Commandos. Later, it was restored and the small cottage beside its entrance gates became a museum: see panel for opening times, which are also posted near its driveway gate.

To make this detour, leave the Way at bullet 5, page 46. After your visit, instead of backtracking, continue past the museum across the white bridge, soon crossing River Arkaig. Turn right along the B8005 and near the hump-backed bridge look for the fine falls where the waters of the Chia-aig drop into the Witch's Cauldron. Return along the Dark Mile (*Mile Dorcha*), a deeply wooded, mossy avenue, to rejoin the Way at Clunes. Following this detour adds about 2 miles (3 km) to the Way. Allow an extra hour or so, or longer if you visit the museum.

> *i* **The Clan Cameron Museum**
> covers the history of the clan and its Jacobite links, and also has photos and artefacts from the commando training era. In 2019 museum admission cost £4. Its gift shop offers tea, coffee and ice cream, and its toilet is accessible. In season, opening hours are normally 11.00 to 16.30. Other visits may be arranged on request. Text or phone 07900 217 975: www.clancameronmuseum.co.uk.

Clan Cameron Museum, Achnacarry

- At Gairlochy locks, turn left across the road bridge, go up the road and follow it around to the right (signed 'Loch Arkaig').

- Soon the Way bears left up a path that runs slightly above the quiet road, rejoining it about 700 m later. Look down to your right to see Gairlochy's pepperpot beacon on the headland.

Shipwreck beside Loch Lochy

- Where the path returns to the road (mile 11·6), cross over and descend on a recently (2019) constructed path to the shore of Loch Lochy. The timber shipwreck on your right is the remains of the former Ballachulish ferry boat – used to dredge the canal after the Ballachulish bridge opened in 1975.

- This charming lochside section runs on a winding path through woodland, past a picnic bench and across several footbridges. Enjoy fine views across and along the loch. The restored Landing Craft was used here during commando training in World War 2.

- At mile 13·3, the lochside path rejoins the road, and you bear right along it. To take the Achnacarry detour, within 500 m turn left at the prominent sign and follow directions on page 45. Otherwise, keep ahead on the road for 1·7 miles (2·7 km) through Bunarkaig to reach Clunes.

- At Clunes, cross the bridge over River Arkaig and turn right along the forest road to an area with picnic benches.

- The route follows a low-level forest track all the way to the farm at Kilfinnan. There are intermittent views of Loch Lochy on your right and small waterfalls on your left.

- At mile 20·1 you reach Glas-dhoire where there's a Trailblazer Rest with composting toilets and space for up to 8 tents. Nearby you may spot the roof of a ruined croft house, inhabited until the 1940s. It's surrounded by rowan trees and probably unsafe to explore.

Glas-dhoire Trailblazer Rest

17

Clunes
Forest

▲
588

Allt Bàn

16

Clunes

Mile Dorcha

B8005

15

60
▲

Abhain Chia-aig

230
▲

Waterfalls ☆

River Arkaig

Bunarkaig

14

☆
Achnacarry
House

B8005

13

Loch Lochy

Allt Coire Chaile-rais

12

Gairlochy
11

47 △ ⌂

- If you keep to the Way it's only 2 miles from Glas-dhoire to Kilfinnan, but if you are taking a day out to climb the Munros above Loch Lochy, start from the signposted track at mile 21·7: see page 27.

- Below the farm is the graveyard with a large mausoleum for the chiefs of the MacDonells of Glengarry. This is a relocated cemetery: before the canal works raised the level of the loch, the bodies were moved from their original position, now underwater.

- From Kilfinnan, the Way is on a minor road. You are close to the site of the Battle of the Shirts (1544). Its name derives from the clansmen's undershirts: it was so hot that they removed their plaids and fought wearing only their undershirts.

- At mile 23, the Way bears right up a driveway and past some chalets, veering towards the small marina, canal and locks. However, the Invergarry Link route stays on the north side of the canal: to follow it, go straight on up the minor road ahead and skip to page 55.

Eagle Barge

The Way crosses the canal at Laggan Locks, which has the Eagle Barge, a Dutch steel barge operating as a floating pub and restaurant, sometimes with live music. There are various accommodation options nearby (B&B, bunkhouse and glamping bothy), and the Lochside Larder (café/take-away) beside Loch Oich on the A82.

Laggan Locks

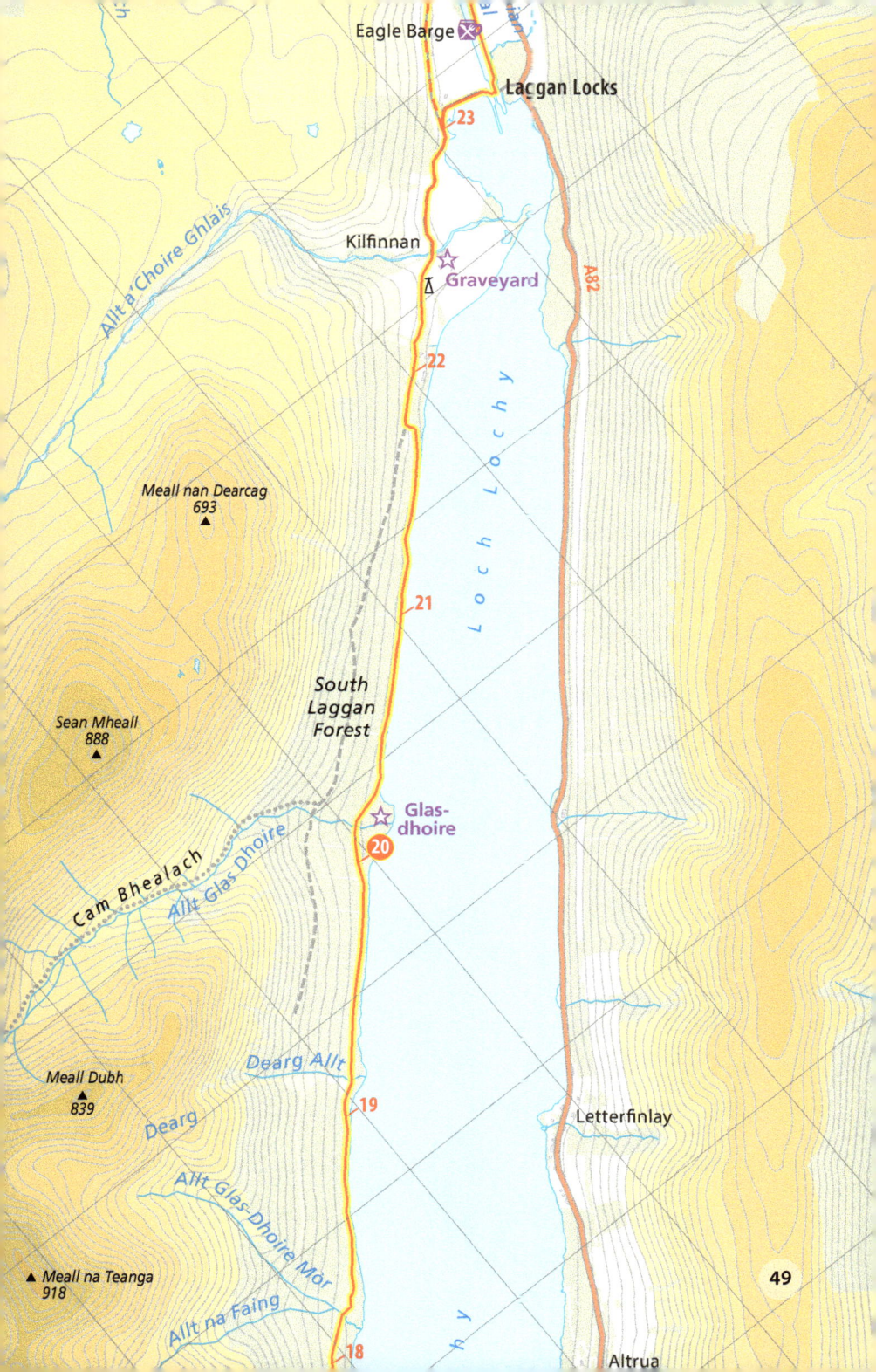

Eagle Barge ⊠

Lacgan Locks

23

Kilfinnan
☆
Graveyard

22

Allt a'Choire Ghlais

Meall nan Dearcag
693
▲

A82

Loch Lochy

21

South
Laggan
Forest

Sean Mheall
888
▲

☆ **Glas-
dhoire**
20

Cam Bhealach

Allt Glas Dhoire

Meall Dubh
839
▲

Dearg Allt

19

Dearg

Letterfinlay

Allt Glas-Dhoire Mòr

▲ Meall na Teanga
918

Allt na Faing

18

Altrua

3·3 Laggan Locks to Fort Augustus

Distance	**11·2 miles 18·0 km**
Terrain	some tarmac, disused railway trackbed, old military road, then canal towpath from Aberchalder to Fort Augustus
Food and drink	Laggan Locks (Eagle Barge): A82 Loch Oich (Lochside Larder); Aberchalder; Fort Augustus (wide range)
Summary	lovely views over Loch Oich (from either route); then passing through mixed woodland to follow charming canalside all the way to Fort Augustus

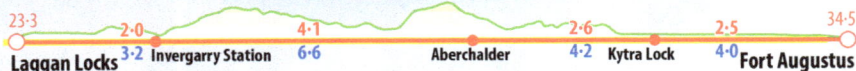

23·3   2·0   4·1   2·6   2·5   34·5

Laggan Locks 3·2 Invergarry Station 6·6   Aberchalder 4·2 Kytra Lock 4·0 **Fort Augustus**

- The Way continues on the towpath with the canal to the left, past tall Scots pines on an embanked section known as Laggan Avenue: see photo below. Telford planted these trees after his navvies had completed the huge task of earth moving by pick and shovel.

- This being the canal's highest section, it runs in a cutting, with good views behind you. The A82 runs parallel to your right, with a B&B and the Great Glen Hostel, host to Active Highs (outdoor activities) nearby. From Laggan Locks to Laggan swing bridge is 1·5 miles (2·4 km) of pleasant towpath.

- At the bridge, you could detour across the canal to the Well of the Seven Heads beside the A82 (about 0·6 miles/1 km each way) if you want to visit this macabre monument or seek take-away food.

- Otherwise, before the swing bridge cross the A82 with care and follow a short road section past the entrance to the Great Glen Water Park (lodges).

- Turn right through a gate to reach the remains of Invergarry station on your right. There's a notice about the restoration project: see the panel on page 51.

Diesel shunter at Invergarry station

Laggan Avenue

Loch Lundie

Lochan Doire Cadha

Aldernaig Burn

☆ **Leiterfearn**

Invergarry Castle

27

Invergarry
ℹ ⊗ 🏪 ⛺ 🏠

A82

Leiterfearn Nature Reserve

26

Creag nan Gobhar
495 ▲

River Garry

△ 🚐

Mandally

Well of the Seven Heads
☆ ✗

Loch Oich

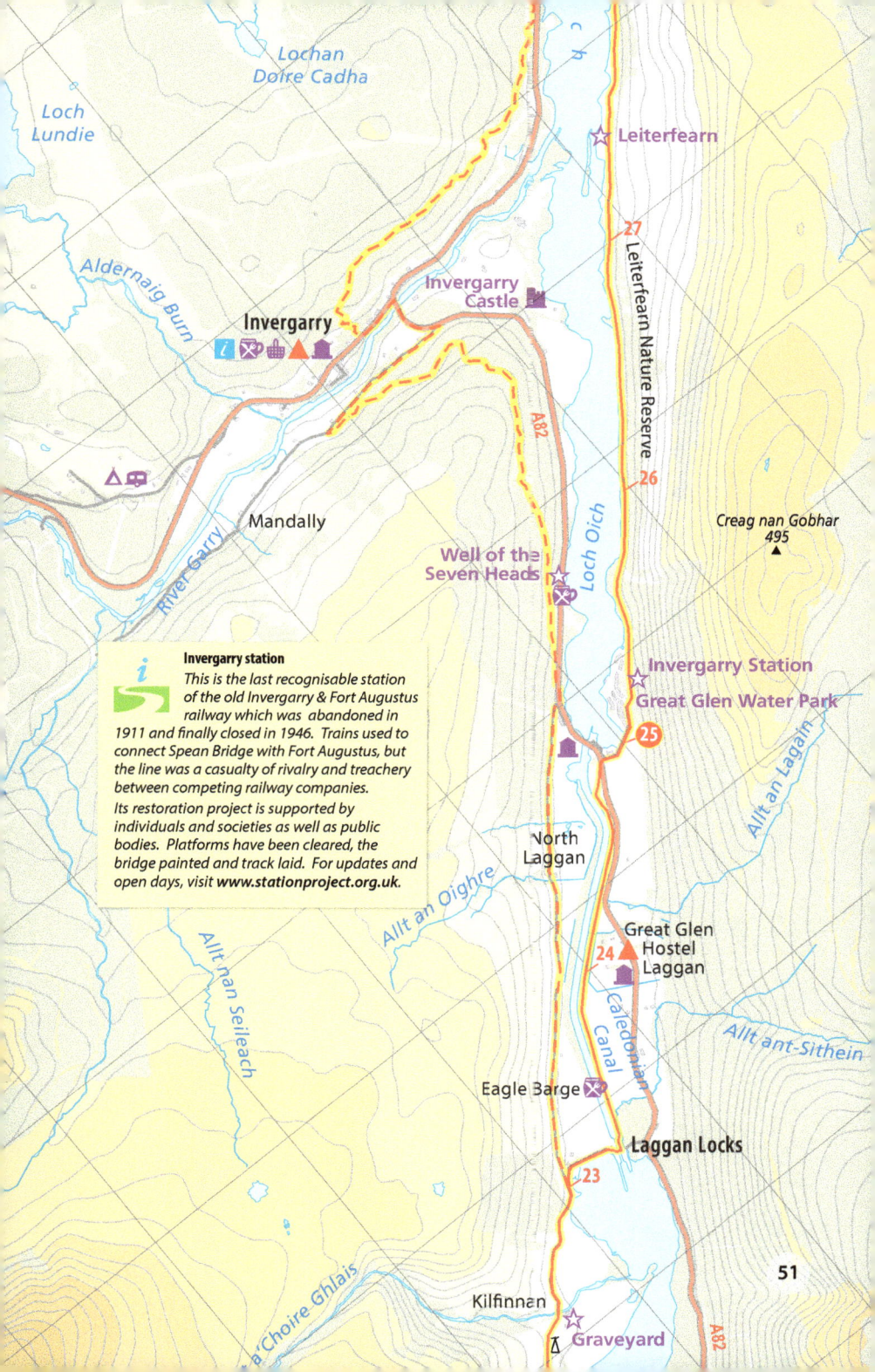

☆ **Invergarry Station**
Great Glen Water Park

25

Allt an Lagain

Invergarry station

ℹ

This is the last recognisable station of the old Invergarry & Fort Augustus railway which was abandoned in 1911 and finally closed in 1946. Trains used to connect Spean Bridge with Fort Augustus, but the line was a casualty of rivalry and treachery between competing railway companies.

Its restoration project is supported by individuals and societies as well as public bodies. Platforms have been cleared, the bridge painted and track laid. For updates and open days, visit www.stationproject.org.uk.

North Laggan

Allt an Oighre

Allt nan Seileach

Great Glen Hostel Laggan
24 ▲ 🏠

Caledonian Canal

Allt ant-Sithein

Eagle Barge ✗

Laggan Locks

23

a' Choire Ghlais

51

Kilfinnan

☆ **Graveyard**

A82

Tunnel carrying the disused railway

- Continue on a track towards the Leiterfearn nature reserve with its wonderful woodland, in spring alive with primrose and dog violets.

- From the station, follow the trackbed beside Loch Oich. At first it runs in a cutting, with no views, but within a mile you start seeing the lovely scenery of Loch Oich.

- Look across to the ruins of Invergarry Castle, nestling in the trees. This was once the seat of the MacDonells who supported the Jacobite cause and hosted Bonnie Prince Charlie. The castle was burned after Culloden.

- The trackbed continues straight and level to Leiterfearn where there is a ruined cottage and a Trailblazer Rest (for up to 8 tents) on the small headland opposite the cottage.

- After Leiterfearn the route continues along the old railway trackbed (also cycleway NCN78), passing through the tunnel shown above.

Yacht heading south into Loch Oich

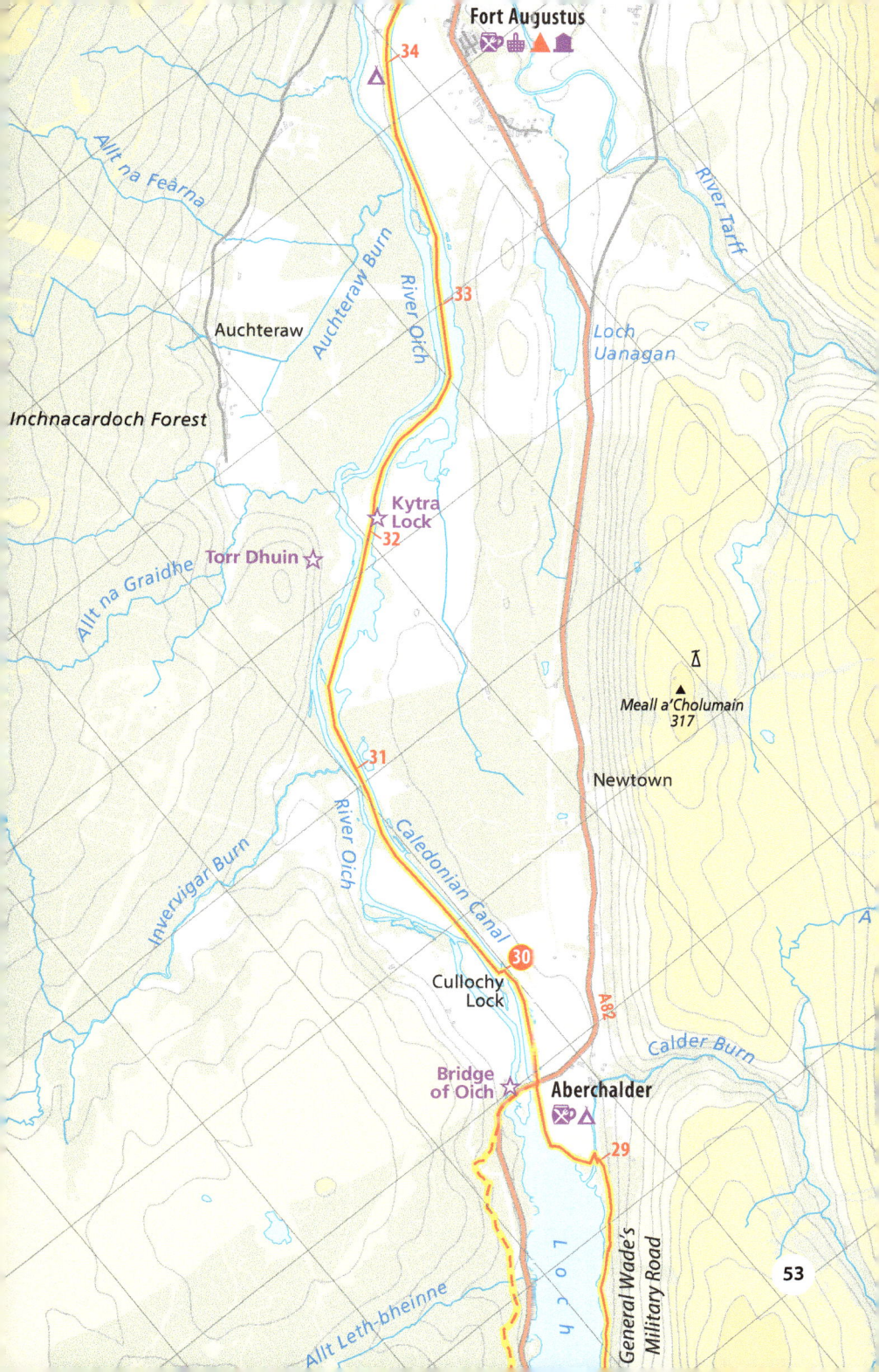

Fort Augustus

34

33

Auchteraw Burn

River Oich

Allt na Fearna

Auchteraw

Inchnacardoch Forest

Loch Uanagan

River Tarff

Kytra Lock

32

Allt na Graidhe

Torr Dhuin ☆

▲
Meall a'Cholumain
317

31

Newtown

River Oich

Caledonian Canal

Invervigar Burn

30

Cullochy Lock

Calder Burn

A82

Bridge of Oich ☆

Aberchalder

29

Loch

General Wade's Military Road

Allt Leth-bheinne

A

Bridge of Oich

- At Aberchalder (pronounced aber-halder), the Way stays on the right side of the canal but it's well worth crossing for a good look at the elegant Bridge of Oich, designed by James Dredge in 1850. Its chains taper towards the middle, and its double-cantilever design makes each half self-supporting. It carried cars until 1932.
- Return from the bridge, and resume the Way with the canal to your left. At mile 30 the Way crosses the canal at Cullochy Lock.
- Enjoy the next 2 miles (3·2 km) along secluded canal through mixed woodland. For much of this section you are on a narrow causeway with canal to your right and River Oich to your left.
- The canal broadens into a narrow natural loch, Loch Kytra. Look up to your left to see Torr Dhuin, the site of an Iron Age hilltop fort: see page 24. To your right you'll see Meall a' Cholumain, a mast-topped hill: see page 30.
- At Kytra Lock there's a small Trailblazer Rest (up to 3 tents). From here to Fort Augustus the Way follows a further 2·5 miles (4 km) of delightful towpath, sandwiched between canal and river. Enjoy it while it lasts: you won't see the canal again until Inverness. The character of the Way changes from Fort Augustus onward.

Cullochy Lock

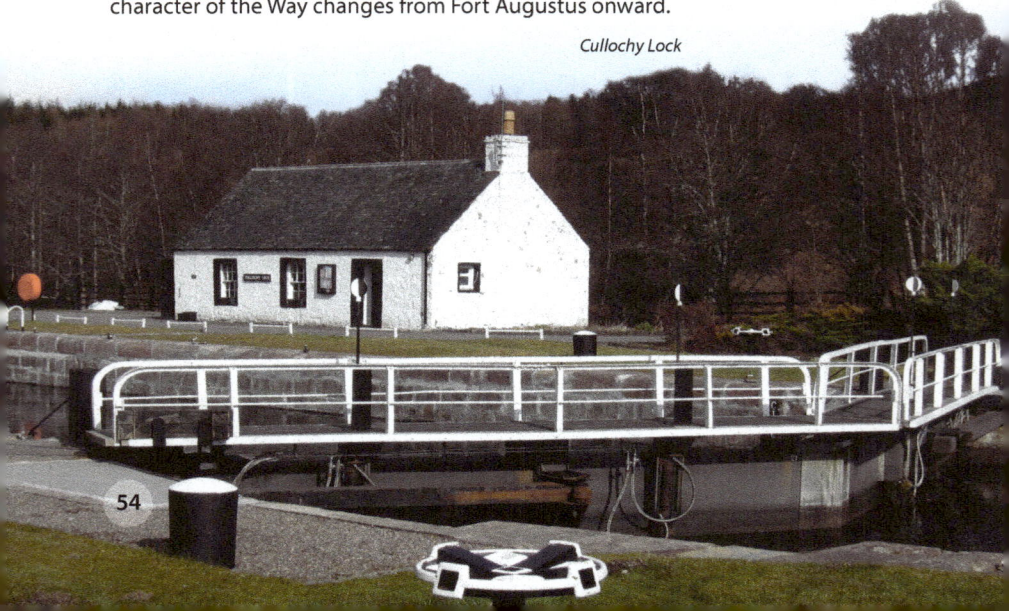

Invergarry Link route

- From mile 23 (page 48, bullet 4) follow the undulating minor road north to meet the A82, with good views north and south.
- Turn left briefly then follow the forest road as it rises steadily through conifer forest. Beyond a junction on the left, you may still see a fine view of Loch Oich and the ruins of old Invergarry Castle, with Loch Ness in the distance.
- Generally descend to a minor road and turn right for 0·6 miles (1 km). Turn left at the A82 and turn left again once across the River Garry. Cross the road and within 100 m of the hotel, turn right up a path to climb steeply to a wide forest road.
- Follow it east and north-east, soon rewarded with a fine view to the south-west of the Loch Lochy hills. Descend almost to the A82, then follow a path which climbs a bit.
- Beyond a footbridge, you're among conifers almost to the A82. For a close look at the splendid old Bridge of Oich, cross the river by the A82 bridge and pass through the canalside car park on your left.
- Afterwards, return to to the A82 and traverse the swing bridge to rejoin the main Way on the far side of the canal. The Link route has a total distance of 8·4 miles (13·6 km).

Fort Augustus

Originally known as Kilcumein, the village was renamed in 1729 by General Wade in honour of William Augustus, Duke of Cumberland. Midway between Fort William and Fort George, Fort Augustus was built in 1729 and became the hub of Wade's network of military roads.

The fort housed troops long after Culloden, until 1867 when it was sold to the Frasers of Lovat, descendants of an executed Jacobite. The 15th Lord Lovat gave it to Benedictine monks who adapted it for use first as a monastery, then as a school and from 1882 as an abbey. After the abbey closed in 1998 the monks moved to Pluscarden. Later it was converted into luxury apartments, self-catering cottages, leisure and sports facilities and a restaurant.

Fort Augustus has many attractions, notably the sight of boats working through the flight of locks at its centre. Visit the Caledonian Canal Centre, on the north side of the canal: open daily year-round (shorter hours out of season), admission free, tel 01463 725 581.

You can cruise Loch Ness with sonar from here year-round: see *www.cruiselochness.com*. There's a waymarked path to the hill fort of Torr Dhuin: see page 24.

The locks, Fort Augustus

3·4 Fort Augustus to Invermoriston

Distance	**7·3 miles 11·8 km**
Terrain	forestry road on Low Route; from Allt na Criche to Invermoriston, option of High Route with its winding path across exposed hillside
Food and drink	Fort Augustus (wide range), Invermoriston
Summary	Low Route runs parallel to Loch Ness' shore with only intermittent views of the water; the more challenging High Route climbs above the trees and offers much better views

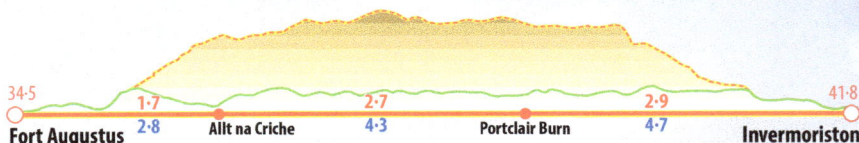

34·5   1·7   2·7   2·9   41·8

Fort Augustus   2·8   Allt na Criche   4·3   Portclair Burn   4·7   **Invermoriston**

- From the main road bridge in Fort Augustus, head north beside the A82 to cross River Oich and pass a garage on the left. Within 200 m bear left up a path leading to a minor road.
- Bear left along the road as it passes the village hall and various B&Bs, and bends right. After 800 m of minor road, at mile 35.3 bear left along a discreetly marked path that climbs steeply through tall conifers to meet a forest road: turn right.
- After the road gains more height, there's a bench with a view over Loch Ness and Loch Ness's only 'island' – actually a crannog, an Iron Age manmade feature. Later it boasted a castle, but now it has only a few trees. It was renamed Cherry Island by Oliver Cromwell.
- At mile 36·1 you reach a waymarked junction with an information board that explains your options. Cyclists may prefer the Low Route, which is less exposed. The High Route appeals more to walkers: it has better views and wildlife, is more strenuous and is slightly longer (by 0·8 miles/1·3 km). Its path leads straight on, soon climbing steeply: see page 58 mid-page.

South over Loch Ness from the Way

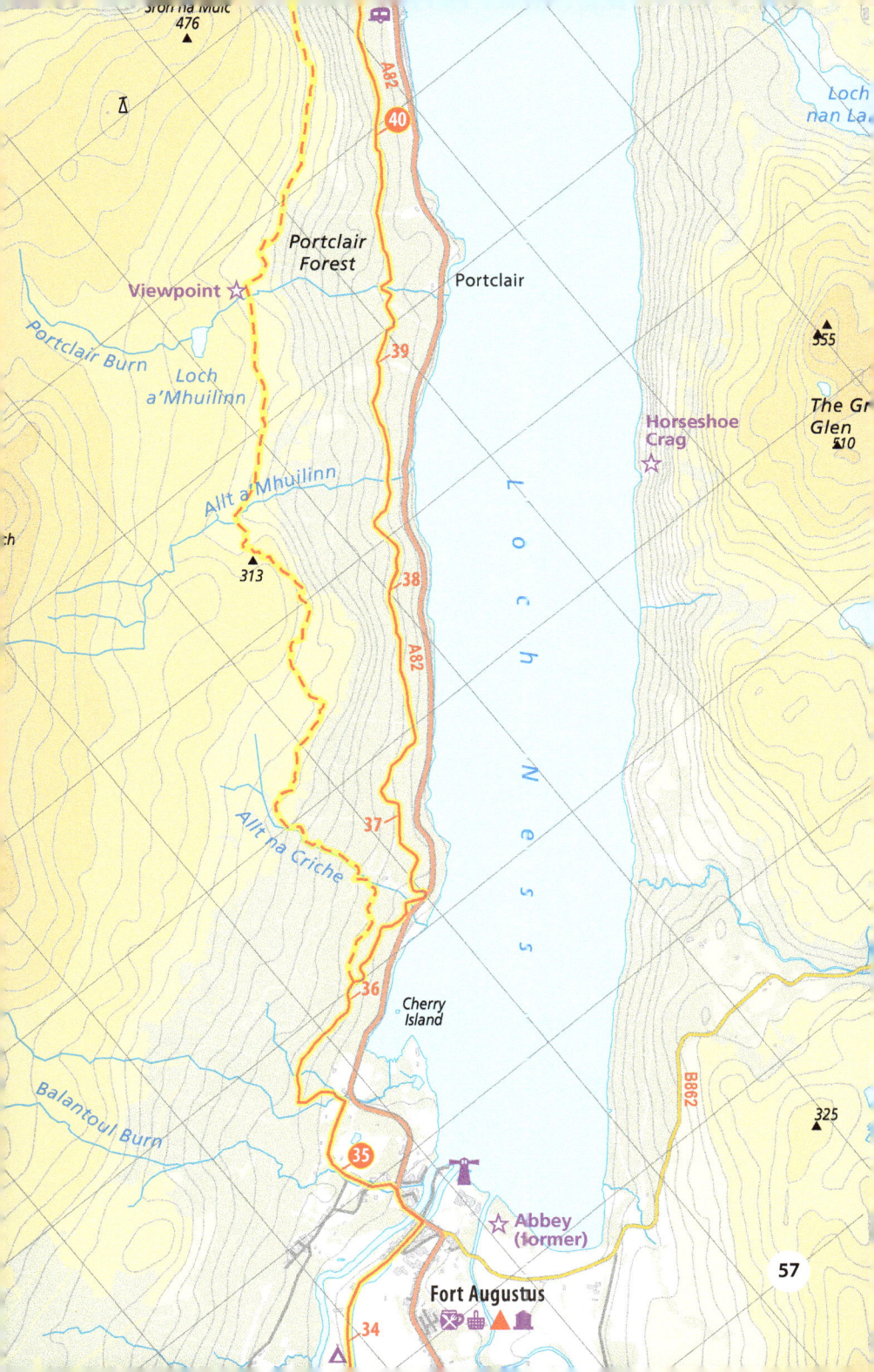

Sron na Muic
476 ▲

A82

40

Portclair
Forest

Portclair

Viewpoint ☆

Portclair Burn

Loch
a'Mhuilinn

39

Allt a'Mhuilinn

313 ▲

Loch
nan La

355 ▲

The Gr
Glen
510

Horseshoe
Crag ☆

L
o
c
h

N
e
s
s

A82

38

37

Allt na Criche

36

Cherry
Island

Balantoul Burn

B862

325 ▲

35

Abbey
(former) ☆

Fort Augustus

34

⌂

Low Route

- The Low Route follows the road bending right downhill in a zigzag almost to loch level. It levels out at about 50 m and crosses the Allt na Criche stream (pronounced alt-na-cree) at a car park.

- It then follows an undulating, winding route through conifer forest for the next 4 miles or so (6-7 km), never rising above the 100 m contour.

- There are breaks in the trees which afford views over Loch Ness, and a number of small waterfalls on the left. You may see the house at Portclair on the lochside, over halfway to Invermoriston.

- After a couple more miles on the forest road, the village of Invermoriston comes into view below. Where the road starts to swing to the left towards Glen Moriston, you are joined from the left by the High Route at mile 41·1.

- Drop down to a path beside the forest road, heading north-west. About 0·6 miles (1 km) beyond the junction, turn sharp right off the forest road down a shortcut path which drops steeply to a minor road.

- Turn right for 500 m, then at the A82 turn left to cross the river and reach Invermoriston. Skip to page 60.

High Route

- From the junction reached at the foot of page 56, the route climbs steeply through the trees for about 800 m on a constructed path, gaining 140 m of altitude in under 1 km.

- When you emerge from the trees, you are richly rewarded with great views back over Fort Augustus. You can trace the curve of the canal and River Oich, and in the distance clearly see Loch Oich perched at a higher level than Loch Ness – the height difference is 164 ft/50 m.

'Snake head' rock feature beside the path

- The path swings north-east and continues to climb, first to 290 m and then to its highest point at 313 m (1030 ft), on the shoulder of Carn an Doire Mhoir. Throughout this section it crosses open ground and offers excellent wide views.

Horseshoe Crag: see top of page 60

Creag Dhearg
526 ▲

Loch a'
Bhealaich
422 ▲

Allt Salgh

Alltsigh
46 —

Creag-nan-
eun Forest

411
▲

45

Creag nan Eun
413 ▲

Meall Doire
Bhrath
359
▲

Allt Coinneag

44

A82

Achnaconeran

43

L
o
c
h

N
e
s
s

River Moriston   A887   42

Invermoriston

Falls, Bridge ☆

41

Sron na Muic
476
▲

A82

40

59

Portclair
Forest

Viewpoint ☆

Portclair

- About mile 38·5, look across the water to the half-oval of bare scree known as Horseshoe Crag. Legend has it that people were trying to lure Nessie out of the loch by putting a bottle of whisky on the hill. The monster is supposed to have taken the whisky, but returned to the deep, leaving the horseshoe trail behind.
- Soon afterwards you reach a splendid curved stone shelter, built at an ideal spot to enjoy the view over Loch Ness.
- There's now a long, winding descent, at first fairly gentle and still with splendid views over Loch Ness. The path crosses Portclair Burn, and descends further, re-entering the trees about mile 40.

The winding descent

- In the forested section, the descent is steep in places, and continues to a junction with a forest road. Cross it and follow a dogleg path down and across another forest road to rejoin the Low Route at mile 41·1: see page 58 bullet 4.

Invermoriston

This little village is centred on the Glenmoriston Arms, built in the 1800s on a site that dates back to a cattle drovers' inn built in 1740. Parts of the very thick granite walls can still be seen inside. The hotel has had many famous visitors since Samuel Johnson and his biographer James Boswell met here on their historic trip to the Hebrides in the 1770s. The village also has a general store and craft shop. There is a drinking water tap outside the Millennium Hall.

The village's early growth was based on timber from Glen Moriston. This was used in the 13th century when ships were built from oak and pine to go on the Crusades. By the 1640s, the village sawmill was in action. In the 19th century, trees were floated downstream for use in constructing the Caledonian Canal. Invermoriston depended on water transport until Thomas Telford built local roads.

Upper falls of Moriston

Telford bridge, Invermoriston

Telford also designed Invermoriston's splendid old bridge. Begun in 1805, its design was sound, but it suffered from construction problems and spiralling costs. Its financer went bankrupt before completion in 1813. The bridge was restored many times, but after flood damage in 1951, it was replaced by the modern bridge (1954) which gives a good vantage point for admiring the older bridge.

The Way crosses the modern road bridge heading north. To see the old Telford bridge properly, descend steps on the far side of the road bridge, cross the old bridge and drop down to view the upper falls. To explore the lower falls, take the woodland path that descends from the east side of the road bridge. There's a summer house with viewing platform overlooking the river where it tumbles down over hard old rocks towards the loch.

From the road bridge, the Way heads towards the Glenmoriston Arms. Steps on your left lead down to St Columba's Well, where the Saint is supposed to have driven out evil spirits and given the water curative powers.

River Moriston, autumn

Distance	15·6 miles 25·1 km
Terrain	Low Route is on forest tracks whereas High Route is on a narrow constructed path; after Grotaig, minor road and roadside path for 3 miles/5 km, with final section on pavement beside the A82
Food and drink	Invermoriston, café at the Grotaig pottery, Drumnadrochit
Side trips	Urquhart Castle, Loch Ness Visitor Centres (two), Loch Ness cruises (various)
Summary	a choice of routes above Loch Ness, with much better views from the more strenuous High Route; easy going on a minor road leads to the descent into Drumnadrochit

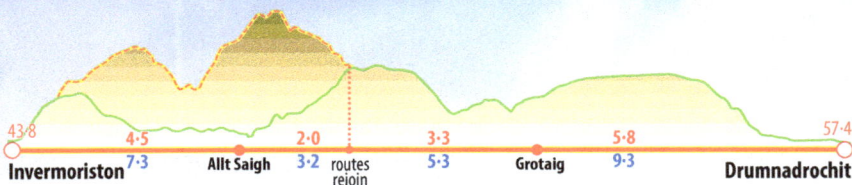

43·8   4·5   2·0   3·3   5·8   57·4

Invermoriston 7·3   **Allt Saigh** 3·2 routes rejoin   5·3   **Grotaig** 9·3   **Drumnadrochit**

- On the north side of the river, face the Glenmoriston Arms Hotel and turn left for 50 m towards the Clog and Craft shop. Turn right up the lane that rises behind it, climbing steeply.
- The road zigzags up to 170 m (560 feet) within 900 m. At a junction with an information board, the High Route goes left, uphill: see page 65.

Low Route

- The Low Route heads right (east), within 800 m crossing a burn, the Allt Coinneag. It then loses half the height you have just attained. You drop down to a forest road and level off at about 85 m (280 feet), starting to enjoy good views over the water.
- A blue post marks a splendid drystone cave which was built in Victorian times by a gamekeeper as shelter for a woman who had to walk regularly from Alltsigh to Invermoriston and back to do washing for the local estate.

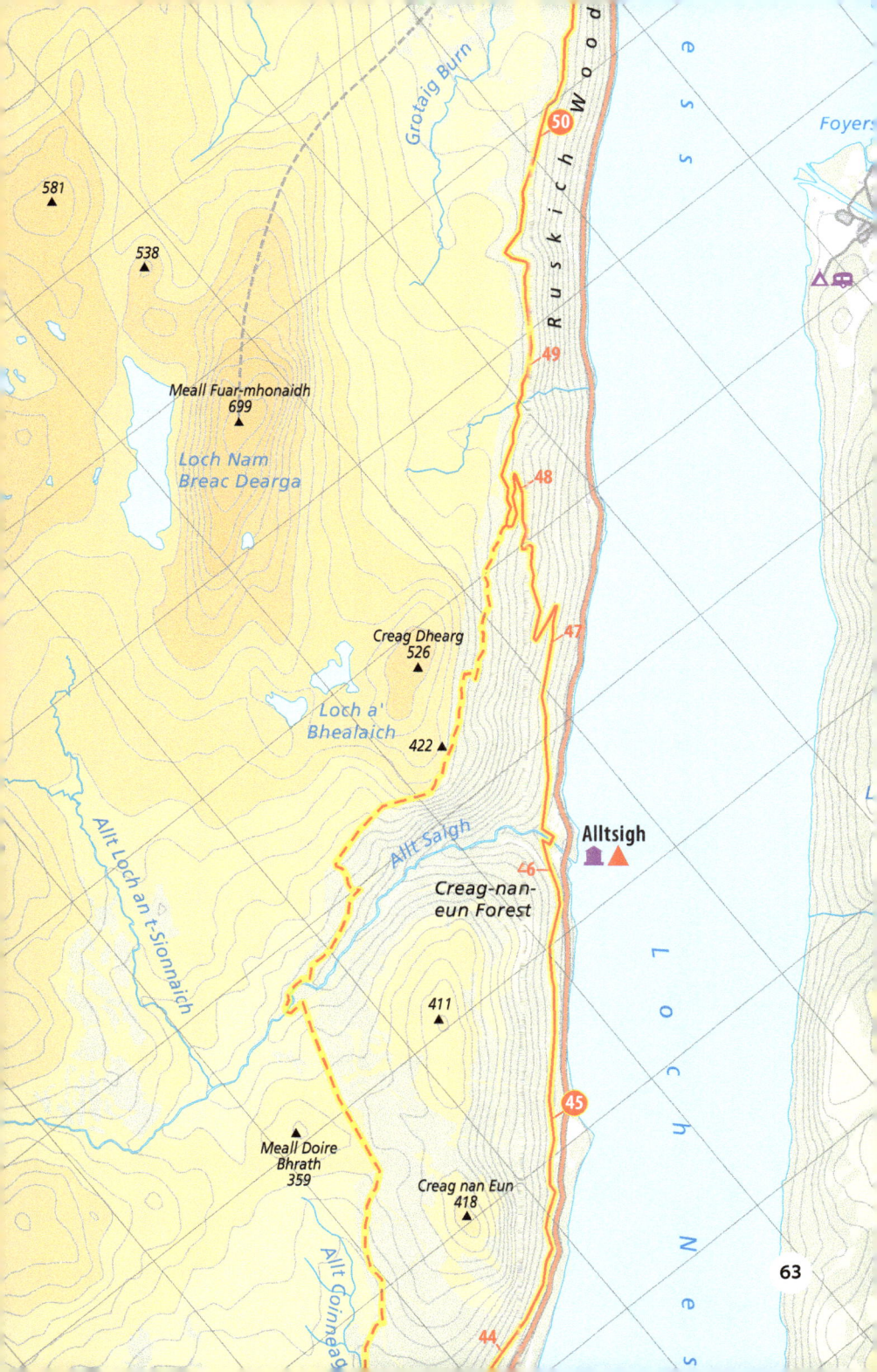

Grotaig Burn

50

Ruskich Wood

581

538

49

Meall Fuar-mhonaidh
699

48

Loch Nam
Breac Dearga

47

Creag Dhearg
526

Loch a'
Bhealaich

422

Alltsigh

Allt Salgh

46

Creag-nan-
eun Forest

Allt Loch an t-Sionnaich

411

Meall Doire
Bhrath
359

45

Creag nan Eun
418

Allt Coinneag

44

Foyers

Loch Ness

- For the next 2 miles (3 km), the forest road runs parallel to the A82, mostly some 30-50 m above it, all the way to the Allt Saigh. Beyond the bridge, to reach the Lochside Hostel turn right to descend to the main road.
- To continue the Way, keep ahead on the forest road. The route climbs to about 300 m (1000 ft), and is joined at mile 48·3 by the High Route.
- From here on, the combined Way undulates on forest road, at first with good views across to Foyers, then through dense forest. It descends to as low as 120 m (400 ft) in Ruskich Wood.
- After going through two gates close together, climb through oakwood and cross a burn via a ford. This takes you up to Grotaig at about 180 m (590 ft).
- At the minor road here, the Way turns right but you may wish to divert left to the café at the pottery. It opens daily for light refreshments, and can provide meals if booked ahead: *www.lochnessclayworks.com*.
- Otherwise, follow the minor road north-east for another 3 miles (5 km) across the plateau. Walkers follow two sections of roadside path. There are good views of Loch Ness to the south-west and Ben Wyvis to the north across fields and moorland.
- In the midst of a harvested plantation, turn left off the road along a wide track to descend to Clunebeg and the River Coiltie. Continue along a gravel road to meet the A82 at mile 56·4.
- To divert to Urquhart Castle, cross the road directly to a roadside footpath. This runs parallel to the A82 and leads to the Castle car park: see page 69. Otherwise, turn left to cross the river at Borlum Bridge. To continue the Way, follow the roadside path to reach Drumnadrochit.
- The Way passes close to Urquhart Bay Wood, an ancient wet woodland around the estuaries of the Rivers Enrick and Coiltie. To explore this, at the crossroads near Borlum Bridge, turn right (east) down the road and go through a gate beside Old Kilmore cemetery. The River Coiltie is not bridged and it may be impossible to reach the loch shore.

Urquhart Bay Wood

High Route

- After the steep climb out of Invermoriston, at the information board (mile 42·5) follow the narrow path uphill through the trees.

- The path soon bends right to climb beside an old stone wall, then swings eastward, still climbing, to emerge above the tree line, offering fine open views to the north and west.

- Within 0·6 miles (1 km), there's a steepish descent on path and stone steps to the Allt Coinneag, which you cross by footbridge. This leads to an easy section on a charming constructed path through birch woodland, climbing gradually.

- The path meets a forest road at a T-junction: turn left and follow it for 0·6 miles (1 km). It narrows to a constructed path, still climbing, through open ground.

- After some zigzags you reach a circular timber viewpoint which invites you to pause and enjoy the distant mountains that it frames: in the photo below, the timber circle encloses the group of Munros just north of Loch Cluanie, some 25 miles (40 km) away, slightly south of west. Further south, to the left of the circle, are Gleouraich and Spidean Mialach, two Munros above Loch Quoich, still further away.

- Afterwards the path continues to climb, levels out and descends to meet a forest road: turn left and follow the road as it swings across a bridge over the Allt Saigh. This stream drops steeply to reach Loch Ness 240 m below, near the hostel on the Low Route.

Viewpoint framing the Munros above Loch Cluanie

- The forest road undulates gently for about 0·6 miles (1 km), then narrows to a constructed path that climbs to a deer fence and then follows it. Soon it reaches a whimsical timber bridge over a burn, known as Troll Bridge and adorned with poems and artwork.

Bridge across the Allt Rhuighe Bhachain

- Over the next 800 m, the path climbs high on the shoulder of Craig Dhearg and is steep, in places very steep. Loch Ness comes into view far below.

- At the highest point of the Way (422 m/1385 ft), there's a splendid horseshoe stone shelter, with the best view yet, not only over the loch but also, on a clear day, for over 40 miles (64 km) to Ben Nevis's north face, with Aonach Mor in front. Behind the shoulder of the nearby hill to the right are the Munros above Loch Lochy (about 30 miles/48 km away).

- Soon after the shelter comes the inevitable long descent. The first section is steep in places, but soon leads to another viewpoint over Loch Ness, with Foyers visible on the far shore of the loch. The S-shaped stone shelter has back-to-back benches, with shelter from any wind direction.

- At mile 48·3, you reach the T-junction with the Low Route, where you turn left. Resume directions from page 64 bullet 2.

South-west from the horseshoe shelter

Abriachan Gardens ☆

briachan
Eco Café 🄐65

Caiplich ☆

Abriachan

Loch
Laide

Allt Loch Laide

Allt Mòr

Carn na Leitire
434 ▲

64

High
Point
382 ☆

63

62

A82

61

L o c h

Meall na h-Eilrig
465 ▲

410 ▲

418 ▲

Loch
Glanaidh

60

N e s s

376 ▲

Drumbuie Burn

59

Temple Pier

*Urquhart
Bay*

58

Allt Tarbh

Strone

Loch Ness
Centre ☆

Drumnadrochit

67

Urquhart
Castle

57

Drumnadrochit

Drumnadrochit is known locally as 'Drum'. Combined with its neighbour Lewiston, the population is about 2000. It hosts various visitor attractions and has a good network of local woodland paths, including Balmacaan and Craigmonie Woodlands. After the closure of the Visitor Information Centre plans were made to replace it with a community-run enterprise in 2020-2021.

Loch Ness Centre

The Loch Ness Centre is a 5-star attraction housed in the Victorian building which was the original Drumnadrochit Hotel. It offers an open-minded approach to the evidence of 'monster' sightings, and its seven themed areas use multimedia to present findings from research and exploration. It's open daily year-round (telephone 01456 450 573). The project also supports an informative website *www.lochness.com* and (from Easter to October) cruises depart hourly on its research vessel.

Nearby, Nessieland has a very different exhibition and is also open daily: *www.nessieland.co.uk*.

Drumnadrochit from the west

Urquhart Castle

Urquhart (pronounced **Urk**-urt) enjoys a majestic situation, commanding fine views along Loch Ness in both directions. It was built around 1250 on the site of an Iron Age fort, for Alan Durward, Lord of Urquhart and son-in-law of King Alexander II. The castle was taken from the English by William Wallace, but Edward I's soldiers recaptured it after a long siege in 1303.

The castle was seized in 1395 by Donald Macdonald, Lord of the Isles, and was besieged, raided and changed hands many times in the 14th to 16th centuries, notably in the Great Raid of 1545. The then owners opposed the Jacobites in 1689, and it was partly blown up by government troops in 1692 to prevent its occupation by surviving rebels. Sadly it was never repaired and much of its stone, timber and lead was plundered as building material.

Many of the present buildings date from the 17th century onward, although earlier parts also survive. The castle was used as a fortress and a residence for over 400 years. Its best-preserved part is the five-storey tower house built in the 16th century by Sir John Grant and known as the Grant Tower.

The castle is very popular, and a routine stop for tourist buses. To enjoy it without the crowds, time your visit carefully, preferably for early morning on a weekday. See page 64 bullet 8 for directions for reaching the castle directly from the Way, and allow plenty of time.

i

Urquhart Castle and Visitor Centre

The castle and its visitor centre are managed by Historic Environment Scotland: www.historicenvironment.scot. The theatre shows a short video on its history, and it also has a shop, museum and café. Admission charge (£12 per adult in 2019) applies even to grounds and café. Open daily year-round from 09.30 (last entry time varies seasonally), telephone 01456 450 551.

Urquhart Castle

3·6 Drumnadrochit to Inverness

71 73 75

Distance	19·6 miles 31·5 km
Terrain	mainly forest and moorland tracks, with several miles on a minor road and finally island and roadside paths
Food and drink	Drumnadrochit, remarkable café at Abriachan, Inverness (wide choice)
Summary	distance makes this section very challenging; if split into two walking days, or cycled, it's much less daunting and features wonderful views; the long descent into Inverness culminates at the castle

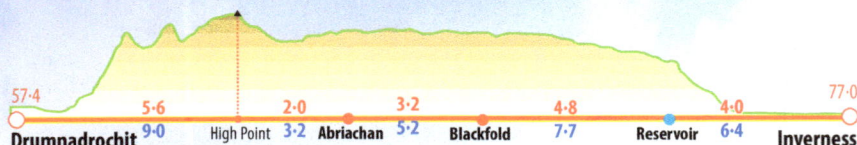

57·4 5·6 2·0 3·2 4·8 4·0 77·0
Drumnadrochit 9·0 High Point 3·2 Abriachan 5·2 Blackfold 7·7 Reservoir 6·4 Inverness

This is a very long section, which many walkers will split over two days. There's lots of variety, with farmland, exposed high moorland and woodland, finishing with the woodland paths of Ness Islands and pavements of Inverness.

- At the centre of Drum, the Way crosses the River Enrick on the A82 bridge and immediately follows the road in a sharp right turn. From here, you follow 1·5 miles (2·4 km) of main road (with pavement): cyclists take extra care on this busy trunk road.
- Just before the private road to Temple Pier, an information board tells the story of John Cobb's tragic attempts in 1952 to set a new world water speed record from here in his speedboat Crusader.
- Immediately after the board, turn left up a narrow path through a gate, to pass around the back of Temple House and garden and resume parallel to the road.
- The path soon starts to climb and passes through woodland. Look behind you for views over Urquhart Castle and the loch, perhaps glimpsing Meall Fuar-mhonaidh to the south-west.
- Soon you enter dense conifer forest, climbing steadily through the trees, with a fine viewpoint on the right offering a last view over Loch Ness.
- The track meets and follows a wide forest road. A board tells the story of the Canadian lumberjacks who volunteered in their thousands to help Britain's World War 2 effort. Inside the box are feedback forms: please help the route managers by completing one.

South-west from the Way above Drum

Abriachan
Eco Café

Abriachan

Loch
Laide

Allt Loch Laide

Allt Loch Laide

Allt Mòr

Carn na Leitire
434 ▲

64

High
Point
382
☆

63

62

Meall na h-Eilrig
465 ▲

A82

61

410 ▲

418 ▲

Loch
Glanaidh

Loch

N

60

e

s

s

376 ▲

Drumbuie Burn

59

Temple Pier

Urquhart
Bay

58

Allt Tarbh

Loch Ness
Centre
☆

Strone

Drumnadrochit
ℹ ⊠ 🏛 △ ▲ 🏠

Urquhart
Castle

A832

Milton

A82

57

△ 🚐

Bor um
Bridge

A831

71

- Look for huge rocks beside the road showing remarkably clear striations – scratches caused by rock fragments scraping past when the glaciers of the last Ice Age retreated.

- The track continues to climb, passing through a mixture of woodland and open moorland but now swinging west and soon leaving the Great Glen for the Abriachan plateau. In a surprisingly flattish part between two rounded hills, this section reaches its highest point of 382 m (1250 ft), marked with a blue post at mile 63.

- The Way then descends slightly to meet a gravel vehicle track near Achpopuli: turn right.

- On your right, it's worth visiting the area where the Abriachan Forest Trust has created a picnic site with eco-toilet, forest school, roundhouse and ark, and a network of paths.

Striations showing glacial action

- At mile 64·6, cross a minor road near Loch Laide, noted for its very pure water. Continue along the narrow path through woodland, punctuated by quaint signs enticing you to visit the Abriachan eco café, trekker hut and campsite on your right (tel 01463 861 462).

- At mile 65·5, the Way meets another minor road and turns left. If you are interested in prehistory, consider turning sharp right first, for a 500-m detour to see the Caiplich prehistoric settlement and field system with 2000-year old hut circles. Retrace your steps to resume the Way along the minor road.

- Follow the road across the Abriachan plateau to mile 67·8, with fine views of the Glen Affric and Strathfarrar hills to the north and west. You may also glimpse Beauly Firth to the north-east.

- About 50 m past an S-bend, turn off along a constructed path which rises gradually across heather moorland, generally parallel to the road at first.

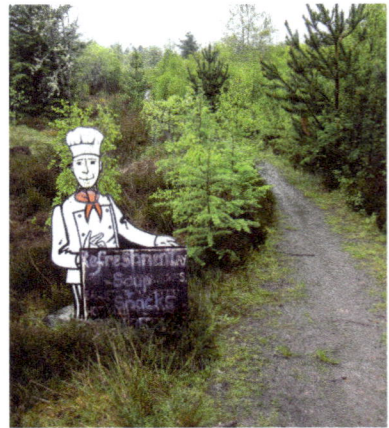
Signage for Abriachan's café

- Continue along the path as it diverges further from the road. The southern outskirts of Inverness soon appear to the east. Clumps of juniper, Scots pine and, further on, tall old larches surround the path, which descends to join a track. Nearby on the right is a useful rendezvous for walkers being collected from Blackfold.

- The Way continues east and turns left through a gate into tall forest. Stay alert for black grouse in this area, which is noted for them. There may be some good views to the north further on through open birch woodland.

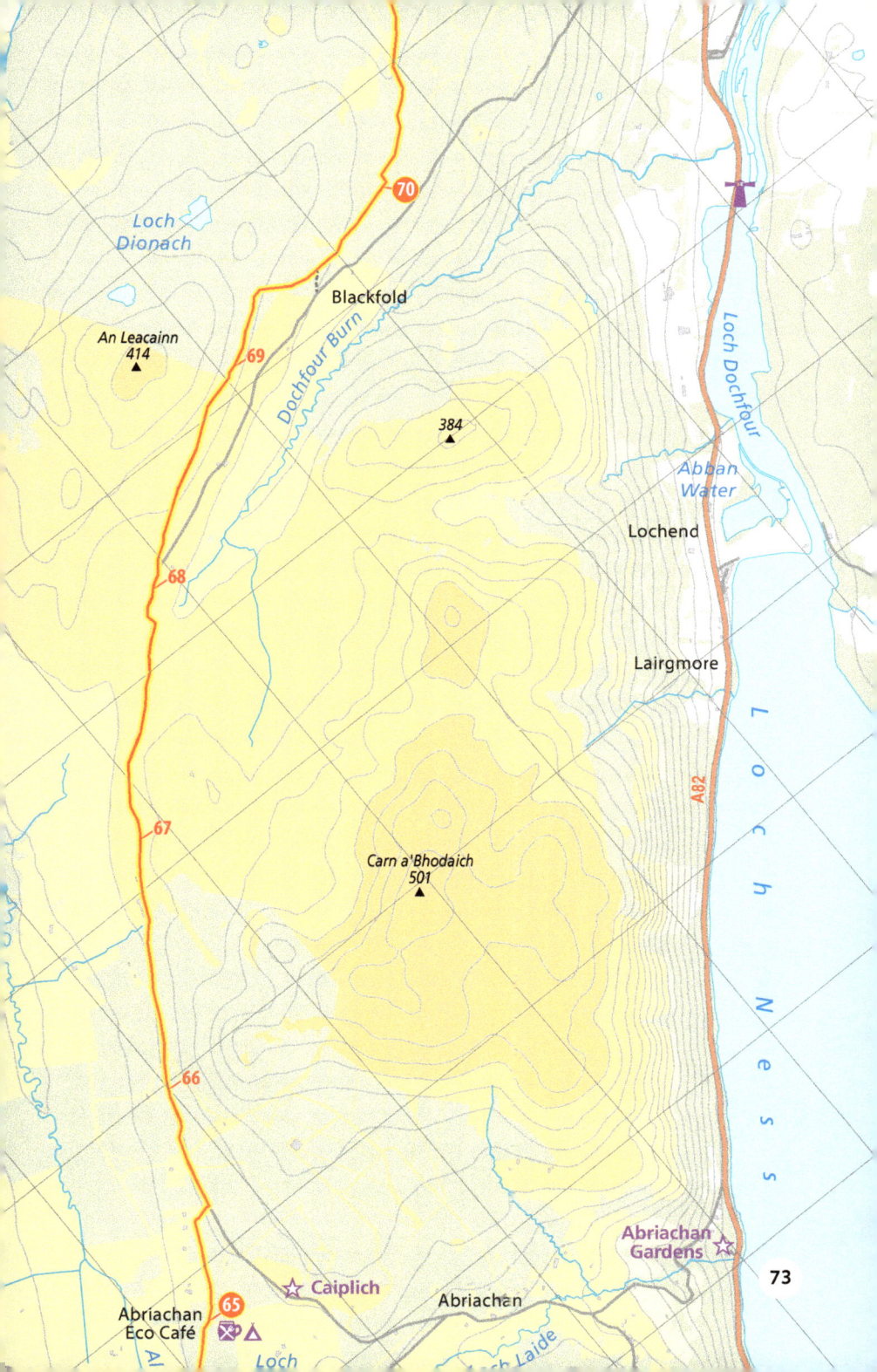

Loch
Dionach

70

Blackfold

An Leacainn
414
▲

69

Dochfour Burn

Loch Dochfour

384
▲

*Abban
Water*

Lochend

68

Lairgmore

67

A82

Carn a'Bhodaich
501
▲

L
o
c
h

N
e
s
s

66

Abriachan
Gardens
☆

73

☆ Càiplich

Abriachan

65

Abriachan
Eco Café

- After nearly 3 miles (4·8 km), turn right along a wide path beneath power lines. Soon, bend left along a path beside a small reservoir (mile 72·9), the haunt of water birds and frogs in spring.
- About 200 m further on, opposite a GGW distance marker, a path leads left up to a clearing around Leachkin chambered cairn, possibly dating from the Neolithic era: see photo opposite.
- Descend across mainly open hillside above the site of the former Craig Dunain mental hospital, which is being developed for housing.
- The path bends right and descends to a gate. Turn left, soon passing the entrance to the community-owned Dunain Woodland.
- Continue down the path, bending right above stone buildings, then left; cross a car park to Forester's Way; cross over and turn left. Bear right along the driveway to Great Glen House, the HQ of Scottish Natural Heritage.
- The Way goes between the building and its car park, then follows a path down the hill. It leads between houses, across open space, then crosses an access road to General Booth Road (mile 74·6).
- Follow the underpass beneath General Booth Road, and go alongside the golf course, past a playing field, to meet the Caledonian Canal for the first time since Fort Augustus. Follow the canalside path to the A82 road, and turn left to cross Tomnahurich Bridge.
- From the far end of the bridge, cross the A82 to join a path beside the canal. Follow it for about 75 m, then turn left down a tarmac path.
- Follow it through two short tunnels and past a car park. Cross a minor road, turn right (the Botanic Gardens is on the left, with refreshments) and continue to Whin Park (toilets).
- Cross the road and follow a tarmac path ahead, soon bearing left to the footbridge over the River Ness. Cross the river to reach Ness Islands and then traverse them to another bridge.
- Once on the east bank, a path between river and road takes you past the Infirmary Footbridge. Continue along Ness Bank: cross to a lane beside a hotel and and follow it to a T-junction. Turn left to go up View Place to reach your destination, Inverness Castle.
- The monument outside the castle is the twin of the one at Fort William, and marks the terminus of the Way.

Congratulations!

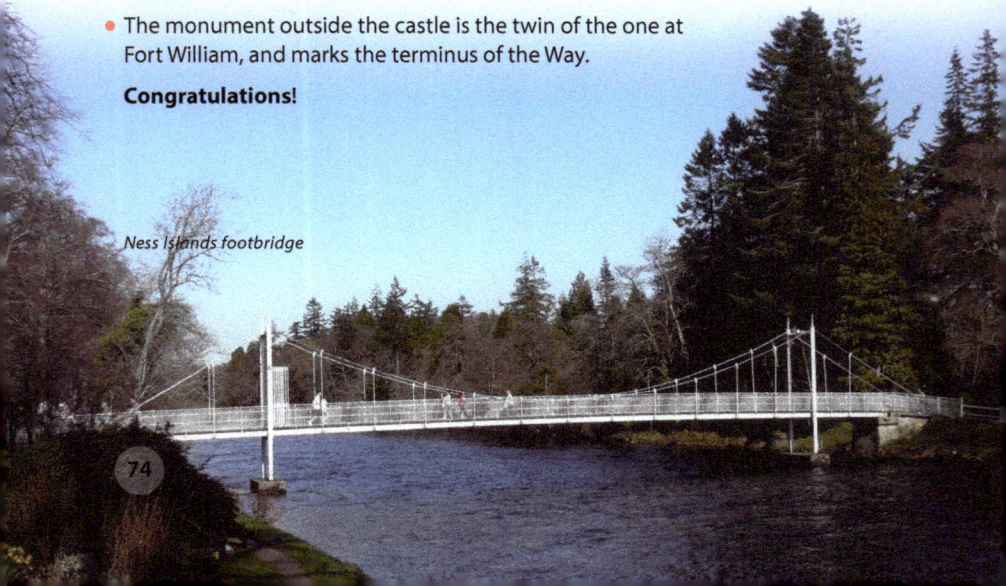

Ness Islands footbridge

North Kessock

Charlestown

Culcab

A9

A96

Mill Burn

A8

B50

B853

Inverness Castle

77

M BU

B861

Inverness

A862

Caledonian Canal

A82

76

B864

Craig Phadrig

75

A8082

Leachkin

74

A8082

Chambered Cairn

73

Reservoir

A82

72

71

Leachkin chambered cairn

Inverness

The site of Inverness has been inhabited for at least 7000 years, and is full of historic interest. Neolithic stone circles and passage-type burial cairns have been found in and near the town. In the 19th century, it benefited from the arrival of the railways and the building of the Caledonian Canal, and many of its fine public buildings are Victorian.

In 1982, there was a further boost to communications in the opening of the Kessock suspension bridge which takes the A9 trunk north across the Beauly Firth. With the expansion of Inverness Airport, it is nowadays well connected by road, rail, water and air.
Always regarded as the 'capital of the Highlands',
Inverness was awarded city status in 2001.

Beauly Firth

Kessock Bridge

A9

A82

Inverness Marina

River Ness

¼   ½ mile
500 m   1 km

N

Clachnaharry sea lock

Muirtown Basin

King Brude Road

Muirtown Bridge

Telford Street

Bus station

Academy St

Rail station

Kenneth Street

Craig Phadrig Hill Fort
see pp24-25

Leachkin Road

Leachkin Brae

Caledonian Canal

St Andrew's Cathedral

Castle

Ness Bank

General Booth Rd

Glenurquhart Road

Tomnahurich Bridge

Kings Golf Course

Sports Centre

Ice Centre

Botanic Gdns

Ness Islands

Great Glen Way

Tunnels

76

A82

2020

Inverness Castle

Inverness Castle stands on the site of various castles dating from the 11th century. It was built of red sandstone to house courts and local government offices. Inverness Sheriff Court moved from here to a new Justice Centre early in 2020. Part of the castle is now the Castle Viewpoint, open daily, where you can climb to a panoramic view.

Nearby in Castle Wynd, there's Inverness Museum and Art Gallery. The museum has displays on the Great Glen, the Caledonian Canal and Highland heritage and folk life, and has a coffee shop. It is open from Tuesday to Saturday (summer), shorter hours in winter (tel 01349 781 730 *highlifehighland.com*).

St Andrew's Cathedral stands beside the River Ness, its twin towers a distinctive landmark. It was founded by Bishop Eden, but designed by the town's Provost, Alexander Ross. Work began in 1866 and by 1869 it had reached almost its present form. Ross had intended 200-foot spires to complete the towers – abandoned because of rising costs.

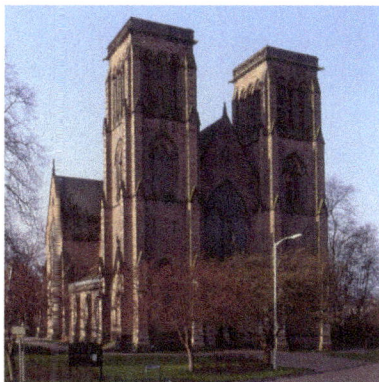
St Andrew's Cathedral

Next to the cathedral is the Eden Court Theatre, a multi-purpose venue for film, concert and theatre, with restaurant. The VisitScotland iCentre is in the High Street, open year-round.

Further afield, you might wish to visit Culloden, the battlefield where the Jacobites were finally defeated in 1746. Its visitor centre is open daily year-round and there's also a restaurant: tel 01463 796 090, *www.nts.org.uk*.

Within the city, consider two expeditions on foot or using public transport. You could enjoy the views from the vitrified fort of Craig Phadrig: see page 24. Or you may wish to complete your 'coast-to-coast' journey by visiting Clachnaharry sea lock: see page 23.

4 Reference

Official website and app

Download the free official Great Glen Way app (Apple/Android) for route updates, interactive maps and listings, or visit the website at
www.highland.gov.uk/greatglenway
To send feedback about the route or any waymarking issues, please email
greatglenway@highland.gov.uk

Accommodation and services

Visit our website for links to Great Glen services, including bike and boat hire, baggage transfer and to companies that offer inclusive holidays, both guided and self-guided:
> *www.rucsacs.com/books/ggw/links*

Scottish Natural Heritage and SOAC

Scottish Natural Heritage is a government body that works in partnership to care for Scotland's natural heritage. Its website is
> *www.nature.scot* and details of the Scottish

Outdoor Access Code are at
www.outdooraccess-scotland.com.

The Code is available as a pocket guide and ebook, and specific advice for dog owners and cyclists is linked from our page
> *www.rucsacs.com/books/ggw*.

Forestry and Land Scotland (FLS)

FLS is responsible for managing and promoting Scotland's national forest estate:
www.forestryandland.gov.scot

Scottish Canals

Website for the body that runs the Caledonian and other canals:
www.scottishcanals.co.uk

The Caledonian Canal operates from 0830 to 1730 on weekdays from Nov-April, and daily from May to October. Sea locks are tidal. The Caledonian Canal Office is at Seatown Marina, Muirtown Wharf, Inverness IV3 5LE tel 01463 725 500.

Visitor Information Centres

The website for Scotland's national tourist board is:
www.visitscotland.com.
Check its sections for Accommodation, See & Do and travel,
> *www.visitscotland.com/see-do/active/*
> *walking*

The VICs (iCentres) at Fort William (tel 01397 701 801) and Inverness (tel 01463 252 401) are open daily year-round, with longer opening hours in season.

The Glengarry Heritage Centre (1 mile from Invergarry) is staffed by volunteers:
> *www.glengarryheritagecentre.com*

In 2019 it was open Easter to October from 11.00-15.00 on Tuesdays-Thursdays only.
High Life Highland operates the Ben Nevis Visitor Centre, with toilets, car park and picnic area: 01349 781 400.

Weather information

The Met Office is the authoritative source on weather in Britain. Visit its website:
www.metoffice.gov.uk or download its app for mobile service. For hill-climbing, refer to the Mountain Weather Information Service website:
www.mwis.org.uk.

Caledonian Discovery

This company offers 6-night cruises on Dutch barges for guests to walk, cycle or canoe the Great Glen, with meals and guiding included. Each barge has just six two-berth cabins, and popular weeks are often fully booked months in advance: phone 01397 772 167 or visit
> *www.caledonian-discovery.co.uk*

Hostels

The Scottish Youth Hostels Association website gives details of hostels and accepts online bookings. Membership is optional, with no upper age limit. Overnight charges range from about £16-£35 per night (plus non-member fee of £3), tel 0345 293 7373.
> *www.syha.org.uk*

Scottish Independent Hostels maintains a list of affiliated independent hostels, see
> *www.hostel-scotland.co.uk*
It produces a useful app with full details and directions: *SiH Hostel Guide*.

Travel and transport

Traveline and Traveline Scotland

For public transport throughout the UK:
> *www.traveline.info*
and throughout Scotland:
> *www.travelinescotland.com*
For both, tel 0871 200 2233 (24 hours).

Buses

Scottish Citylink (buses)
> *www.citylink.co.uk*
Stagecoach (buses)
www.stagecoachbus.com and choose Highlands.

Train travel and tickets
> *www.scotrail.co.uk*

Flights

easyJet *www.easyjet.com*
flybe *www.flybe.com*
KLM *www.klm.com*
Inverness Airport
> *www.invernessairport.co.uk*

Notes for novices

For those who lack experience in long-distance walking, we have prepared notes on choosing and using gear. Visit our website: *www.rucsacs.com* and scroll to foot of page for *Notes for novices*. Cyclists can gain advice from Cycling Scotland *www.cyclingscotland.org*, CTC Scotland *www.ctc.org.uk/scotland* and Sustrans *www.sustrans.org.uk*.

Other useful websites

The Loch Ness Project maintains a good archive on the scientific explorations of Loch Ness:
www.lochnessproject.org
Historic Environment Scotland provides helpful information about heritage, including Inverlochy and Urquhart Castles:
www.historicenvironment.scot
It also maintains a valuable database on Scotland's archaeology and heritage, including the Great Glen hill forts:
www.canmore.org.uk
National Trust for Scotland
www.nts.org.uk

Pests and managing them

For a midge forecast, visit
www.smidgeup.com
The NHS provides info about ticks and Lyme disease here:
www.nhs.uk/conditions/lyme-disease/

Useful links

For links to a wide range of relevant websites for anybody who walks, cycles or paddles the Way:
www.rucsacs.com/books/ggw/links

Ben Nevis

If you plan to climb Ben Nevis, check the Mountaineering Scotland website for a detailed description, for safety advice and how to navigate across the plateau to/from the summit:
www.mountaineering.scot/activities/hillwalking/ben-nevis

Further reading

Cameron, A D (2005) *The Caledonian Canal* Birlinn 236pp 978-1-84158-403-4
Well-researched and detailed account of the history of the canal

Hutton, Guthrie (2009) *Caledonian, the Monster Canal* Stenlake 56pp
978-1-840334-50-9. Plenty of photos supported by concise text

Owen, Kirsty *Urquhart Castle: the Official Souvenir Guide* 48 pp, direct from Historic Environment Scotland's online shop.

Shine, Adrian (2006) *Loch Ness* Loch Ness Project 32pp 978-0-955311-0-5. Generously illustrated account of scientific research and monster sightings

Maps: printed and online

The maps in this guidebook are more than adequate to follow the Way, which is well waymarked. For side-trips and hillwalking you may need a larger-scale map. Footprint publishes a waterproof route map *Great Glen Way (2nd ed)* at 1:40,000 which (in 2019) cost £9.95 (978-1-8711149-94-4).

Harvey also publishes a waterproof *Great Glen Way* route map at 1:40,000 (printed on XT40 polythene) which costs £14.50. Be sure to get the latest edition. The Way is also covered by Ordnance Survey Explorer maps at a scale of 1:25,000.

Please visit our online route map at
www.rucsacs.com/routemap/ggw
and zoom in for amazing detail. This shows the entire route very accurately, and also marks points of interest

Acknowledgements

We are very grateful to all who commented on drafts of this and earlier editions, especially Bruce Kocjan, George Duff and Phil Waite of Highland Council; to Forestry and Land Scotland and Phil Thompson for early access to the High Route; to Caledonian Discovery, especially Adam Wall, for route details. None of them is responsible for our opinions, nor for any errors that may remain.

Photo credits

John Allan p64; **Sandra Bardwell** p7l, p9 (four), p20, p24, p25, p27, p30, p56, p68l, p70, p74, p75, p76, p77l; **Paddy Dillon** p31, p44l, p46l, p52u; **Dave Kelly**/Geograph.co.uk p71; **Jacquetta Megarry** title page, p7u, p8, p9 (five), p13, p14, p21, p22 (both), p23, p26, p28 (both), p39, p40 (all three), p42u, p45, p46u, p48 (both), p50u, 54 (both), 58 (both), 60 (both), p62, p65, p66 (both), p68u, p72 (both); **Sandy Morrison** p36 (both); **NERC Satellite Receiving Station**, University of Dundee p19; **Andrew Pointer** back cover; **Hal Skinner** p23u; **topshotUK**/istockphoto.com p32u; **VisitScotland** p44u and p77l;
www.coolcamping.com p10; *www.lochness.com* p18 (all); *www.macsadventure.com* p5; *www.scotaviaimages.co.uk* p16.
We thank **Dreamstime.com** and its photographers for the following images: **Thomas Lukassek** front cover; **Moodda** p4; **Paula Gent** p17; **Josefkubes** p28; **Steve Allen** p32l; **Andrew Astbury** p33u; **Brian Kushner** p33l; **Mikelane45** p34; **12qwerty** p35u; **Dbeatson** p35l; **Maxim Pyshnyy** p37u; **Eric Mandre** p37l; **David Dennis** p38; **Debsta75** p42l and p69 **Alan5766** p50l; **Peewam** p52l; **Petr Švec** p55; **Karen Appleyard** p61u; **Ollie Taylor** p61l.

Index

Units

Distances are shown in kilometres and miles, and heights in metres only.

These rules-of-thumb give rough equivalents:

- to convert metres to feet, multiply by 3 then round up by 10%
- to convert km to miles, divide by 2 then round up by 25%.

Map scale and contours

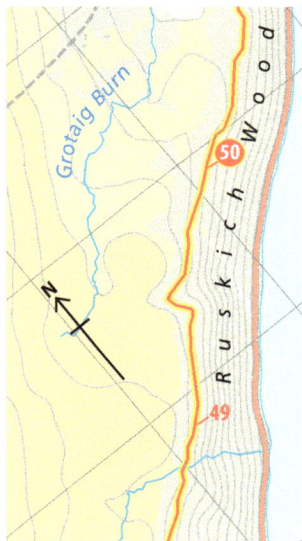

About the mapping

Map scale is 1:38,000 and cumulative distance from Fort William is shown in miles. The grid lines are at 1 km intervals. The contour interval is 25 m (82 ft) with a change of colour every 100 m (328 ft). Spot heights are shown in metres.

Map pages have north rotated by 39° anti-clockwise.

⊗ Lovell Johns®

The mapping in this book is © Rucksack Readers, commissioned from Lovell Johns Ltd, a leading mapping company that has served public and private sectors for over 50 years: *www.lovelljohns.com*

Key to maps

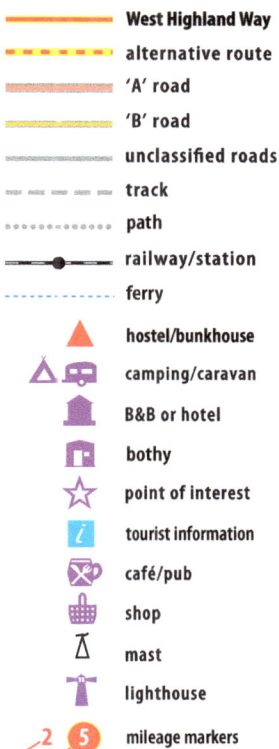

▬▬▬	**West Highland Way**
▬ ▬ ▬	alternative route
▬▬▬	'A' road
▬▬▬	'B' road
▬▬▬	unclassified roads
▬ ▬ ▬ ▬	track
··········	path
▬●▬	railway/station
- - - - -	ferry

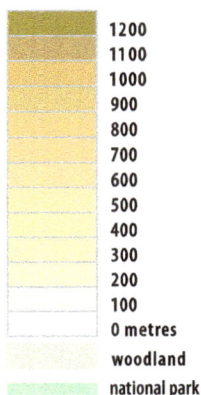

▲	hostel/bunkhouse
△ 🚐	camping/caravan
🏛	B&B or hotel
🏠	bothy
☆	point of interest
i	tourist information
☕	café/pub
🧺	shop
⊼	mast
🗼	lighthouse
2 ⑤	mileage markers

	1200
	1100
	1000
	900
	800
	700
	600
	500
	400
	300
	200
	100
	0 metres
	woodland
	national park

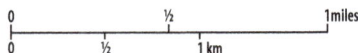

Great Glen Way: Official Rucksack Reader

This POD edition was created in 2020, based on the sixth, fully revised edition of our rainproof guidebook.

Rucksack Readers,
6 Old Church Lane, Edinburgh, EH15 3PX, UK

tel	+44/0 131 661 0262
email	info@rucsacs.com
web	*www.rucsacs.com*

ISBN 978-1-898481-94-2

British Library cataloguing in publication data: a catalogue record for this book is available from the British Library.

Designed in Scotland by Ian Clydesdale (*www.workhorse.scot*)

Mapping is © Rucksack Readers and was created specially for this book by Lovell Johns. It contains Ordnance Survey data © Crown copyright and database rights 2020 with further material collected by the authors.

Town plans based on mapping by Wendy Price Cartographic Services with information from the Royal Commission on the Ancient and Historical Monuments of Scotland (RCAHMS).

Publisher's note

All information was checked prior to publication. However, changes are inevitable: take local advice and look out for signage e.g. for temporary diversions. Walkers and cyclists should check two websites for updates before setting out: *www.rucsacs.com/books/ggw* and *www.highland.gov.uk/greatglenway*

The weather in the Highlands is unpredictable, and some parts of the Way are exposed and remote. Do not rely on having mobile phone reception. You are responsible for your own safety, and for ensuring that your clothing, food and equipment are suited to your needs. The publisher cannot accept any liability for any ill-health, accident or loss arising directly or indirectly from reading this book.

Feedback is welcome and will be rewarded

We appreciate comments and suggestions. All feedback will be foloowed up, and if comments lead to changes, readers will be entitled to claim a free copy of our next edition upon publication. Please email us at *info@rucsacs.com*.

Visit our website :

Great Glen Way
(6th ed)
£13.99

Jacqueline Mowatt, Sandra Bardwell

"Robust, waterproof, comprehensive and enjoyable ... an essential companion". - Undiscovered Scotland

The Great Glen Way runs for 77 miles (124 km) along Scotland's historic Great Glen between Fort William and Inverness. It follows the historic Caledonian Canal and runs beside four of the Highlands' loveliest lochs. These include Loch Ness, famous for its monster legend and for Urquhart Castle.

This 6th edition of our popular guidebook was fully revised after extensive fieldwork on the High Route in 2014, and further revised in 2016. If you have a previous version, we recommend you to download section 3.3 and section 3.4 which were both rewritten, with new photographs.

All readers are recommended to download pages 64-65 for the change resulting from the completion of the Inverness bypass in 2016.

Visit the website for zoomable route map, links and support services

Rucksack Readers

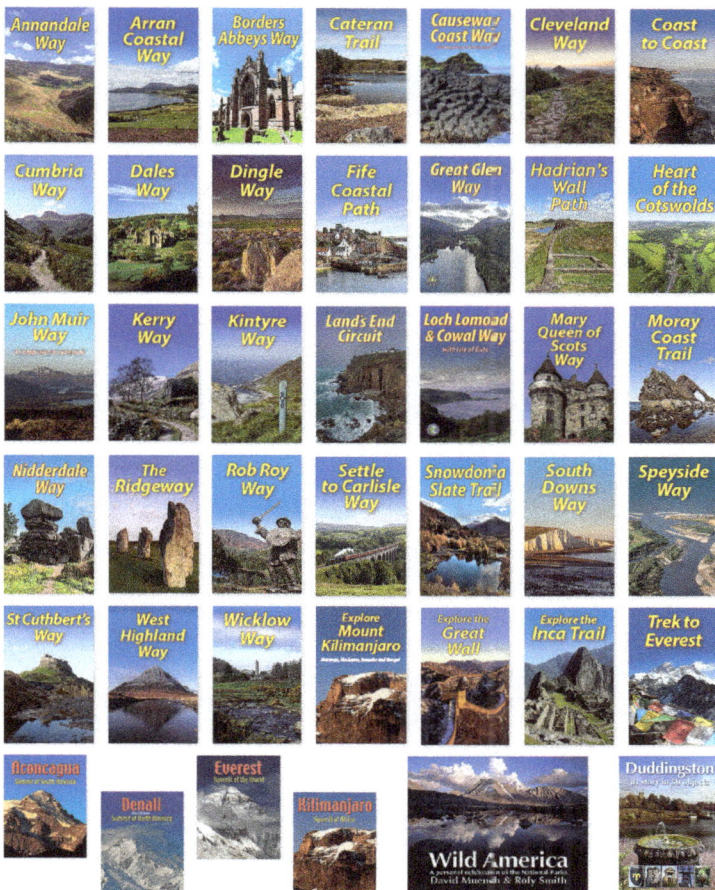

Rucksack Readers has published books covering long-distance walks in the UK, Ireland and worldwide (the Alps, China, Peru and Tanzania). Its series *Rucksack Pocket Summits* is for climbers of the world's 'seven summits'. For more information, or to order online, visit *www.rucsacs.com*. To order by telephone, dial 0131 661 0262 (outside UK dial +44 131 661 0262).

www.ingramcontent.com/pod-product-compliance
Lightning Source LLC
Chambersburg PA
CBHW051213090426

42742CB00021B/3439